D0894328

Enigma Books

Also published by Enigma Books

Sergio I. Minerbi

The Eichmann Trial Diary

Translated by Robert L. Miller

Enigma Books

EMMA S. CLARK MEMORIAL LIBRARY
Setauket. L.I.. New York 11733

All rights reserved under International and Pan-American
Copyright Conventions.
No part of this publication may be reproduced, stored in a retrieval system,
or transmitted, in any form or by any means, electronic, mechanical,
photocopying, recording, or otherwise without permission of Enigma Books.

Published by
Enigma Books
New York.

Original Italian title:
Eichmann. Diario del processo

Copyright © 2000 and 2011 by Sergio I. Minerbi
Copyright © 2011 by Enigma Books for the English translation

Translated by Robert L. Miller

First English-Language Edition

Printed in the United States of America

ISBN 978-1-936274-21-5
e-ISBN 978-1-936274-22-2

Publisher's Cataloging-In-Publication Data

Minerbi, Sergio I.
 [Eichmann. English]
 The Eichmann trial diary / Sergio I. Minerbi ; translated by Robert L. Miller. -- 1st
English-language ed.

 p. ; cm.

 ISBN: 978-1-936274-21-5
 eISBN: 978-1-936274-22-2

 1. Eichmann, Adolf, 1906-1962--Trials, litigation, etc. 2. War crime trials--
Jerusalem. I. Miller, Robert L. (Robert Lawrence), 1945- II. Title. III. Title:
Eichmann. English

KMK44.E33 M5613 2011
341.690268/05694

Contents

Preface

Fifty years have passed since the trial of Adolf Eichmann, the SS officer who was in charge of every detail in the implementation of the infamous Holocaust that Adolf Hitler had decided against the Jewish people in Europe. Interest in this case, however, from every point of view, appears to be growing, all over the world, from year to year. The persecution of the Jews had also been mentioned in a number of well-known cases, like the Nuremberg Trials, but in those proceedings the Holocaust perpetrated against the Jewish people was always only a marginal point, or was only partially mentioned and described. The Eichmann trial, on the other hand, covered these terrible happenings from every angle, because the defendant was in charge of the department of the Gestapo dealing with Jewish matters throughout the Second World War.

The reports in this book, covering the daily proceedings of highly important pieces of evidence and developments during the trial, held in Jerusalem, Israel, in 1961, were written and prepared by Dr. Sergio Itzhak Minerbi, who attended each daily court session.

Dr. Minerbi was born in Italy and arrived in what was then Palestine in 1947; he became the local correspondent of Italian national radio, R.A.I., in 1960. He happened to be in Rome when the president of Argentina, Arturo Frondizi, announced the kidnapping of Adolf Eichmann, who was taken from Argentina to Israel. On the same day the author signed a contract with the Italian publishing house

Longanesi for a book about the trial that would follow Eichmann's capture.

During the trial Dr. Minerbi covered all the proceedings for Italian radio and television, and two years later those daily reports were published in Italian in a book called *La Belva in gabbia* (The Caged Beast) which was the code used by the Mossad to inform Prime Minister David Ben Gurion that Eichmann had been captured. This book is the English translation of the original Italian publication.

The daily description given by Dr. Minerbi, covers the most important and devastating pieces of evidence, Eichmann's reactions, the special remarks made by the judges, the discussions in court, the legal, moral and factual problems in the case. It all makes for fascinating reading, and is bound to impress the reader far more than the formal court record of the proceedings or any updated analysis of this historical trial.

Gabriel Bach
former State Attorney of Israel
and former Justice of the Israeli Supreme Court

Introduction

Adolf Eichmann was one of the leading officials involved in implementing the Nazi policy to kill the Jews during the Second World War.

According to the Nazi terminology used at the time, the policy was known as "the final solution to the Jewish problem." Adolf Hitler, the founder and leader of the Nazi movement, clearly stated his anti-Semitism in his book *Mein Kampf* (My Struggle) and began enacting his views as soon as he became the German Chancellor on January 30, 1933. After having promulgated a number of anti-Jewish laws, on the evening of November 9, 1938, using as an excuse the murder of a German diplomat, Ernst von Rath, in Paris, the SS burned synagogues and other Jewish buildings, destroyed six thousand Jewish-owned stores and murdered at least 100 Jews, while thousands more were arrested and sent to concentration camps. The avowed purpose was to eliminate the Jews from the German economy, expel Jewish pupils from the schools, and enforce compulsory emigration from Germany. Acting on Hitler's orders, Hermann Göring demanded that "the Jewish Question be coordinated and resolved one way or another." The *Zentralstelle für die jüdische Auswanderung* (Central Agency for Jewish Emigration) was set up in January 1939. In the course of a meeting that took place one month later and chaired by Reinhard Heydrich, all issues pertaining to the Jews were placed under the jurisdiction of the German police.

Heinrich Müller, the head of the Gestapo, was appointed chief of the main office and he in turn appointed Adolf Eichmann, who was then transferred from the SD to the political police. This office was known as RSHA *Amt* IV; Eichmann was also the head of the Emigration and Evacuation Department (IV B 4), which was later renamed Jewish Issues and Evacuation. In that capacity Eichmann organized the forced emigration that a few months later became a euphemism for deportation to the death camps.[1] In September 1939, at the beginning of the Second World War, Adolf Hitler made the decision to kill the Jews of Poland.

At the end of the war Eichmann fled from Germany and went into hiding in Argentina, using a false identity; he was identified and captured by the Mossad on May 11, 1960, then taken to Israel. In the course of his trial, which opened in Jerusalem on April 11, 1961, he could have chosen to either voice some regret as a man who understood the enormity of the crimes that had been perpetrated or he could play the role of the arrogant SS lieutenant colonel who would express his displeasure at having been unable to complete his murderous mission. Instead, perhaps to strengthen his own defense, he decided to claim having only played a minor role as someone who only acted *im auftrage* or under orders issued by his superiors. This position, which he took during the trial, is clearly expressed in his final statement as well: "I had the misfortune of being involved in those horrors even though they were not the result of decisions I made. It was never my intention to kill people. It was only the political leadership that was responsible for the collective murders. […] My only fault was one of obedience, of respect for discipline, a soldier's duty in wartime as well as the oath I had taken as a soldier and a civil servant."

This line of defense is contradicted by historical facts since Eichmann was not an ordinary civil servant but one of the key officials in

---

1. Lucy Davidowicz, *The War Against the Jews, 1933–1945* (London, 1975).

the Nazi hierarchy and therefore directly responsible for the deportation of the Jews to the death camps.

The verdict was handed down on December 15, 1961, and Eichmann was hanged on May 31, 1962.

The original title of this book was *La Belva in gabbia* (The Caged Beast), which happened to be the code word used by the Mossad to inform Prime Minister David Ben Gurion that Eichmann had been captured.

This book was written in real time as the events were unfolding and is mostly based upon the radio and television broadcasts that I was making from the courthouse for RAI-TV (Italian State Radio and Television.)

Many new books have appeared since then, among them Hannah Arendt's well-known work about Eichmann;[2] the study by the chief prosecutor at the trial, Gideon Hausner;[3] the psychiatric evaluation of Eichmann; the many books recently published on the Holocaust;[4] and finally in August 1999 Adolf Eichmann's own memoirs made public by the Israeli State Archives during the trial for libel in the action brought by David Irving against Professor Deborah Lipstadt and Penguin Books publishers in London.

The London Trial

The London Court ruled against David Irving on April 11, 2000. He had initiated a legal action for libel against Deborah Lipstadt and her publisher. The issue to be decided in the case was a crucial one since, among other matters, it also involved Irving's Holocaust denial

---

2. Hannah Arendt, *Eichmann in Jerusalem: A Report on the Banality of Evil* (New York: Penguin, 1964)

3. Gideon Hausner, *Justice à Jerusalem. Eichmann devant les juges* (Paris, 1966). *Justice in Jerusalem* (London: Nelson, 1967).

4. For example see Wolfgang Benz, *L'Olocausto* (Turin, 1988). *The Holocaust: A German Historian Examines Genocide* (New York: Columbia, 2000); Bruno Segre *La Shoah. Il Genocidio degli ebrei d'Europa* (Milan, 1998); Anne Grynberg, *Shoah. Gli ebrei e la catastrofe* (Milan, 1995); Hans Safrian, *Eichmann's Men* (Cambridge: Cambridge, 2010); Michel Onfray, *Le Songe d'Eichmann* (Paris: Galilée, 2008); David Cesarani *Becoming Eichmann: Rethinking the Life, Crimes and Trial of a "Desk Murderer"* (New York: Da Capo Press, 2006); Harry Mulisch, *Criminal Case 40/61, The Trial of Adolf Eichmann: An Eyewitness Account* (Philadelphia: University of Pennsylvania Press, 2005); Haim Gouri, *Facing the Glass Booth: The Jerusalem Trial of Adolf Eichmann* (Detroit: Wayne State University Press, 2004); Hanna Yablonka, *The State of Israel vs. Adolf Eichmann* (New York: Schocken Books, 2004).

positions. In the course of some thirty books Irving had written a number of absurdities: that Adolf Hitler had not planned the extermination of the European Jews and that the killings that did take place were not systematic, among other statements. The contrary was true but Irving claimed that Hitler had never ordered the murder of the Jews and that he had even attempted to put an end to the massacre. At the trial Irving introduced a document, which, according to him, was an order from Hitler to not liquidate thirty thousand Jews sent from Germany to Latvia in November 1941. Actually Irving had doctored the translation of the document to show that the order had been issued by Hitler. He also stated that the execution by shooting of one and a half million Jews on Germany's eastern borders with the Soviet Union did not originate from a coordinated plan but was the result of a series of gross mistakes that Hitler was unaware of.

The defense was able to prove that Hitler had personally approved the orders to kill. For example, in an order dated August 1, 1941, to a mobile unit, an *Einsatzgruppen,* it was written that Hitler was receiving continuous reports on the killings being carried out by that same unit. Irving was then forced to admit that a report from December 1942 confirming the details of the execution of 363,211 Jews in Southern Russia, the Ukraine, and in Bialystok "had in all probability been shown to Hitler."

During the trial Irving claimed that the Nazis may have killed between one and four million people but not in any systematic way and without using gas chambers. In a speech he had given some time before in Calgary, Canada, he had denied that an extermination camp existed at Auschwitz, stating: "It's nonsense, a legend. I can state that more women died in the back seat of Edward Kennedy's car at Chappaquiddick than in a gas chamber at Auschwitz."

In handing down the sentence, Judge Charles Gray pointed out that Irving was motivated by his anti-Semitism and his pro-Nazi positions and that he had willfully falsified history in order to exonerate Adolf Hitler from his responsibility in the extermination. Deborah Lipstadt was able to show that Irving had consistently and deliberately falsified and modified the historical evidence in order to make it fit into his ideas. The judge established that Irving "for his own ideological reasons had persistently and deliberately falsified and manipulated historical proof; and that for the same reasons and without justification had portrayed Hitler in a favorable light mainly with respect to his attitude toward the Jews and his responsibility in the way the Jews were treated."[5] The judge added: "It is my conclusion that no objective and honest historian has any reason to doubt that gas chambers did exist at Auschwitz and that they had been used extensively to kill hundreds of thousands of Jews."[6]

We have mentioned the London trial of David Irving because it was on that occasion that the defense was able to obtain the diaries of Adolf Eichmann from the Israeli State Archives, where Hitler's personal role in directing the so-called "Final Solution," or the physical elimination of the Jews, was clearly stated.

A Psychiatric Assessment

Following the publication of the Eichmann memoir, the psychiatric study of his personality ordered by the Israeli prosecution was also made public. Professor I. Shlomo Kulczar, who was born in Budapest in 1901 and died in 1984, was in charge of the examination and had left the file among his papers that were kept by his son, Adam Kozer.[7] The psychiatrist administered seven tests to Eichmann, from January 20 to March 1, 1961.

Kulczar then sent the test results to one of his colleagues, a Swiss psychiatrist, without revealing the patient's name. Dr. Leopold Szondi of Zurich replied on April 1, 1961, that although he would not ordinarily offer a diagnosis in the dark, "his impression was that the patient [had] an obsession with killing." On November 18, 1963, Szondi wrote: "It is tragic how in this case the patient had tendencies that resulted in a tragedy, a destructive form of thinking with his

---

5. "Irving Consigned to History as a Racist Liar," *The Guardian*, April 12, 2000.
6. See also Valentina Pisany *L'irritante questione delle camera a gas. Logica del negazionismo.* (Milan, 1998)
7. Ran Edelist, *A Look Into Satan's Soul* (in Hebrew), *Maariv*, March 2000, p.10.

defense mechanisms so weak that they left him completely at the mercy of his instincts."

Kulczar's conclusion was: "[Eichmann] is an ambitious sadomasochist with an average-to-good intellect, devoid of any moral values, who acts under the influence of his egocentric and impulsive emotions and attempts to find a real and rational justification to his actions instead of seeking moral approval. The motivations of his personality are to be found in the complex relationship with his father figure. That relationship signals that to be weak and passive is dangerous; he may and actually must prove his virility through forceful positions and actions. In a certain way those relations can be explained by his formal adaptation to doing what is asked of him while he actually rebels and follows his own will."

Eichmann had "an obsession about killing" and that was the reason he fulfilled his task with such fervor and loyalty to Nazism; one might say almost with pleasure.

The False Gods

Goedzen or *The False Gods* is the title that Eichmann chose for the book he wrote while he was in prison in Israel following his trial and before being sentenced. Historians are divided in their assessment of the importance of Eichmann's memoirs. The dean of Holocaust studies at the University of Vermont, American historian Raul Hilberg, was among the enthusiasts: "Even if he omitted something to protect himself—which is only natural—one can say that 98 to 99 percent of what he wrote is true." Prof. Yehuda Bauer on the other hand feels that Eichmann's memoirs have no historical value and that there is a danger if they are read in isolation, that they might create a distorted impression of the Holocaust: "Someone who comes to this without any prior knowledge and takes this memoir seriously will be making a mistake because he should read the trial transcripts instead."[8]

---

8. Elli Wohlgelernter, "Memory and the Nazi Master Plan," *The Jerusalem Post,* March 3, 2000, p. 35.

Judge Gabriel Bach, who was part of the prosecution team at the Jerusalem trial and had read the memoirs very carefully, thinks that they do not add anything to the testimony of the witnesses and the transcripts. Israeli journalist Tom Segev wrote that the manuscript's importance resides mostly in the insights it offers into the thinking of a war criminal such as Eichmann.

Eichmann wrote those memoirs on his own initiative during the four months between the end of the trial proceedings and the sentencing and he wanted them published immediately, but Ben Gurion decided that the book should be withheld for fifteen years. A few excerpts were published by Hausner in his book about the trial. The entire text covers about 1200 handwritten pages and it was the third time that Eichmann was offering an autobiographical description of his life.

The first such description came in a long taped interview in Argentina in 1957 given to the Dutch journalist Willem Antonius Maria Sassen from the newspaper *Der Weg*. For the most part the interview, conducted over the course of five months, was transcribed into 659 pages and introduced by the prosecution at the Jerusalem trial, but the judges didn't allow it to be added to the record because the original tapes were missing. Besides, as Eichmann told Sassen: "The Roman Catholic Church? I never heard it raise its voice loud enough, in any case not enough for me to feel compelled to pay any attention."[9]

During the pretrial period in Jerusalem, Eichmann spoke to Chief Inspector Abner Less, who gave the protocols to the chief prosecutor and then published them in a book.[10] The memoirs were released to the public on February 29, 2000, from the Israeli State Archives in Jerusalem. Today anyone may access them in German on the internet[11] and it is clear at the outset that they will not yield any surprises. The memoirs however are useful to clear up some key details and above all to better understand the personality and thinking of a top Nazi official

---

9. See Hausner *op. cit.* p. 336.
10. Pierre Joffroy et Karin Konigseder, *Eichmann par Eichmann*, Preface by A. Less (Paris, 1970).
11. See the site www.nizkor.org

and through him an entire generation of young Nazis. According to Tom Segev the memoirs do not strengthen Hannah Arendt's thesis of the "banality of evil" since Eichmann was anything but an ordinary man: he was a Nazi true believer, a zealot who was convinced that obedience was the overarching value system and who goes on to explain at length to his readers why he couldn't escape, resign, or rebel.

Even noted historian Barbara Tuchman writes that: "Eichmann was no ordinary man and his case does not belong in any way to what has been called the "banality" of evil. That the author of that extra-ordinary sentence could allow herself to be seduced in such a way by Eichmann's self portrait is one of the mysteries of contemporary journalism. Coming from a woman who calls herself an historian it defies description. [...] He was nothing but a civil servant, wedded to his *routine,* who obeyed orders: that was the defense that Eichmann used and maintained throughout all his interrogations and during his trial. [...] To choose such a defense strategy derives either from a bottomless form of naiveté or the conscious desire to come to Eich-mann's defense which is even more incredible."[12]

The memoirs are also helpful in the struggle against Holocaust deniers since they provide a detailed description of the Nazi bureau-cracy as it was set up to murder the Jews. As a top Nazi official, per Eichmann's own account, he personally visited the locations where the genocide was taking place.[13] His memoirs, much like the earlier ones by Rudolf Höss,[14] point to the enormous risk implicit in blind obedience to what were "clearly illegal orders."

In his memoirs Eichmann lingers at length on this crucial point of his defense and writes: "The issue of guilt feelings is one of the most difficult to answer and in responding I must underscore the difference between the legal side and clarify the human side of guilt. First of all the acts for which I am being prosecuted have to do with my participa-tion in the deportations. Since at the time these took place this was a political order, I am convinced that legal guilt can fall only on the per-

---

12. Barbara Tuchman, "Introduction" to Hausner *op. cit.,* p. 19.
13. Tom Segev, "Adolf Eichmann's Gods" (in Hebrew) *Haaretz,* March 3, 2000.
14. Rudolf Höss, *Commandant of Auschwitz* (London: Phoenix, 2000).

son responsible for the political decision. Where there was no responsibility there was also no guilt. Therefore the consequence of my argument is that responsibility must be ascertained from the legal standpoint. Until we find a global solution to human coexistence from the political point of view, order and obedience remain the cornerstones of any kind of order."

While tirelessly repeating that his duty consisted in obedience without any moral considerations, without ever voicing any doubts about any of the orders he was given, Eichmann provides us with a portrait of the model Nazi civil servant, bound by his duty, capable of conveying the Jews to the death camps just as easily as if he were shipping potatoes to the army's warehouses. Yet a flash of some form of humanity did exist within him. In January 1943 Gestapo chief Heinrich Müller sent Eichmann to Chelmno, near Poznan in Poland, to report back on the killing of Jews that was taking place there. Eichmann wrote in his memoirs:

> What I witnessed there was pure cruelty. I saw naked Jewish men and women enter into a bus that had no windows. The doors were shut and the engine was revved up. The exhaust fumes were channeled back inside the bus. A doctor wearing his white smock had me watch through the window on the driver's side to witness the operation. At that point I couldn't bear it. I cannot find the words to describe my reaction to such things. Everything seemed unreal. I believe that I was able to control myself. I was unable to fulfill Müller's order to time the killings. I just forgot about it and would have been incapable of doing so physically. The bus then began to move. I followed up to a point in the forest and when we arrived the bus stopped near the edge of a pit that had already been prepared. The doors were opened and the dead bodies rolled, one over the other, into the pit. I had seen all of them alive just before and now they were all dead. Then a civilian jumped into the pit and opened their mouths to remove their gold teeth with a pair of pliers.

Eichmann would like us to believe that he was moved by the sight of the corpses, but what actions did this prompt him to take? He certainly didn't ask for a change in his assignment or to be sent to the front in order to avoid being involved in organizing the killings. No, not at all. He only made sure that he wasn't watching; he followed his orders and forgot the ugly scenes by drowning them in alcohol.

Author's Note to the Reader

This book was written as a daily diary and is therefore not divided into specific chapters. The boldface titles within parts of the text refer to the appropriate headings of Chief Prosecutor Gideon Hausner's summation.

The Eichmann Trial Diary

Friday April 7, 1961

Drenched and yet indifferent to the heavy rain that is falling today, perhaps for the last time this season, a few religious Jews wearing their holiday hats covered in fur are standing very close to *Beit Haam*, the People's House. Eichmann has been held inside for three days but the news was only made public now.

On Tuesday night a strange looking ambulance arrived secretly in Jerusalem with its headlights turned off and a heavy police escort. It was the armored vehicle that took Adolf Eichmann from the "Yiar" prison near Haifa, where he was being held since his arrival in Israel until he was transferred to the top floor of *Beit Haam*. Zero hour is very close now: in a few days one of the two great trials of the century is about to begin. In the courtyard, protected by a very high metal fence and on the roofs of the houses nearby, the border police in their typical green caps and submachine guns are watching.

What are these old men with their locks of hair dripping with water and their grey beards flowing over their black caftans thinking? Perhaps, as is their custom, they are once again making the connection between this event and the Holy Scriptures.

Eight days before the whole Jewish family, including the most distant relatives, came together to celebrate Passover and their freedom from Egypt and the treacherous Pharaoh. Three thousand years have passed yet that event is remembered every year since that time, as it is written: "Each one must think of himself as having left Egypt." And those old men have no doubts that it is so: all they need to do is to think of Eichmann locked up in his cell to reach the conclusion that God has once again delivered them from their latest tyrant.

Yet, as Israeli prime minister David Ben Gurion stated, there is a deeper reason that made such a trial necessary. "Young Israelis," he said, "must be made aware. They don't realize that those who were killed were the best part of our people that gave scientists and philosophers, poets, and physicists to the world. But this trial is also important to the rest of the world. If it is true that Nazi Germany bears a heavy responsibility, it is also true that England, France, and the

United States could have saved thousands of Jews and did not do so. Humanity must be reminded what anti-Semitic madness can lead to because it could reappear tomorrow somewhere else."

It is the youth that is the main source of concern. The *Sabras* born in Israel are accustomed to defending themselves with weapons and to retaliate, at times desperately, against those who are attacking them. What do they know about Nazi extermination? Little or nothing. A few facts learned at school, a few abstract figures, all end up losing any kind of meaning and it becomes sometimes difficult to make the difference between events that took place fifteen years ago from those of the past two hundred or two thousand years. This is particularly true in a country where the millennia tend to overlap one another.

The question that the younger generation asks most often is: "Why didn't the European Jews revolt and resist using weapons rather than being butchered so passively?" It is precisely the question that drives crazy the survivors who knew what Auschwitz was all about. The camp where, as the writer Kazetnik stated, everyone was hoping that death would stop when his turn came, that the crematorium door would stay shut exactly when the moment arrived to be reduced to a pile of ashes.

People have the most widely divergent opinions. A driver who became impatient because of three roadblocks on the streets near *Beit Haam* told me: "Wouldn't it have been better to get rid of him down in Argentina? We would have avoided all these complications. First of all there is the diplomatic tension with Argentina that became offended even though Buenos Aires is crawling with Nazis. Then came the call at the UN Security Council. Then Parliament found that a special law had to be passed to allow Servatius coming in as a foreign attorney to serve as the defense lawyer. Then we had to pass another law to carry out a possible death sentence: since its founding the State of Israel had never carried out a death sentence. In one word a whole series of useless complications, don't you think?"

Monday, April 10

The preparations were being completed to get the *Beit Haam* building and its fixtures ready. Workers were running around everywhere soldering pipes, nailing pieces of wood, and setting up the telex machines. The building was originally meant to have a theater, a gym, and a few smaller rooms for municipal cultural activities. However, with the sudden need to find space that could hold five hundred journalists and a small group of spectators and diplomats led to the conversion of the theater into a courtroom and the gym into a press room.

The structure is far from imposing, even though the windowless northern side could be vaguely reminiscent of an old Roman fortress. Security measures were apparent everywhere, in particular at the entrance. Each person entering will have to be frisked in one of the twelve cement cubicles that have been specially built for that purpose; they must leave all packages and bags in a special check room and must show a picture identity card validated with rubber stamps. These measures cannot be considered exaggerated given the number of people who would like to silence Eichmann out of fear or to seek revenge.

Television and news cameras will be allowed in the courtroom despite the opposition of defense attorney Robert Servatius. The number of cameramen however will be kept to a minimum.

The newsmen in the press room will be able to connect their tape recorders to an internal line leading into the judges' and witnesses' microphones and can follow the questioning on several closed-circuit television screens. A special post office was set up to handle all telexes, cables, and international phone calls. Besides this organizational effort there will also be simultaneous translation of the proceedings and questioning and the court transcripts will be published in English, French, and German, as well as the official language, Hebrew.

While they are waiting for news items that are not yet available, the newsmen crowding the press room are all very restless and try to kill time and justify their presence some two thousand or more miles away from home. The bad luck of being affected by sun spots spares no one and makes communications even more difficult. Each one reacts according to his disposition; G. is angry because the telex machine doesn't work; Rome doesn't answer and he thinks his messages should be diverted to Paris, Bern, and Geneva. He attempts unsuccessfully to explain to a stone-faced employee (but how can we know how much he is suffering behind his impassive mask?) the conundrum of tele-communications and his newspaper's needs. Then suddenly, once the perforated yellow strips of the telex machine finally perk up again, G. is brought back to life by all the clatter and looks fondly at the mechanical device with a warm paternal eye. It puts him in such a good mood that he tells his colleagues a joke.

Then there is T., who is very serious and never loses his temper and barely shows any concern due to the absence of any real news or the phone call to be placed two hours later that will inevitably be disrupted by electric static. He manages to dictate his piece over the phone in good time and after that takes a deep breath, yet he always remains unruffled, never losing his reserve with only a faint smile crossing his lips.

Tuesday, April 11

The trial begins on a Tuesday, which in truth feels just like any other Tuesday. Not far away, at the Bezalel Art School, the girls are rushing to their classes carrying huge art folders. They will be busy drawing Corinthian columns or Ionian arches all day, just as they were yesterday and will be again tomorrow. It's still early. The tight alleyways of the Zihronot[15] district nearby, built some eighty years ago, are an ultra-religious neighborhood. On the cobbled stone streets children wearing long locks of hair that stick out from under their *yarmulkas* are playing along with girls in long stockings that reach all the way up their thighs. The men must already be inside the seminaries where they study the scriptures for days on end. These children in the streets, the face of a housewife peeking furtively out the window with her wig covered with a kerchief, the beards that appear mysteriously in the dark room of a synagogue—it could well be the Jewish quarter of Warsaw. A corner of the Diaspora, that same Diaspora that Eichmann had so methodically destroyed, seems to have resurfaced.

Facing the *Beit Haam* a woman is looking out the window as she hangs her clothes to dry. The blazing sun reminds one of springtime romps in the country rather than of criminals locked up in a cage.

---

15. "The memories"

Beit Haam: the People's House. A name that is filled with meaning. There is an entire people standing behind the judges today: a dead people which is no less powerful for it. The trial proceedings may follow every prescribed rule but it is impossible to prevent the victims from being present in the courtroom and weighing in over the prosecutor, the judges, and the newsmen. They are present for everyone except the defendant, who stated during the examination before trial that he had no regrets; he used the same cold efficiency to send people to their deaths as if he'd been managing a spare parts warehouse.

We enter the courtroom. The judges will come in and sit very shortly on the stage of this small theater. One step lower there will be two official translators and to the right the court stenographers. Further down to the left there is a bullet proof glass booth, closed on three sides, where the defendant will sit with his jailers. He will be able to communicate with his defense attorney by using a headset just as he had done previously in prison. In front there is the witness stand. Below that comes the long table of the defense attorneys and the prosecutors. A double barrier sets apart the first seats used by the audience. Four invisible television cameras will record the proceedings using miles of videotape.

Beit Hamishpat! "The Court!" are the words cried out by an aging usher with a very professional voice announcing the entrance of the judges. The hall is filled to capacity and appears to shudder in unison. Everyone rises, including the defendant who was brought into the booth almost furtively. We have been waiting for months to see him in the flesh: the super criminal, Adolf Eichmann. Now that he has appeared silently, once the judges sat down in their chairs, we almost didn't notice his arrival: the drama of the moment was lost. Possibly because of the ordinary, flat, almost insignificant appearance of Eichmann himself.

Moshe Landau, the presiding judge of this court, begins by reading the indictment. The defendant stands at attention. "Are you Adolf, son of Adolf Eichmann?" the presiding judge asks. "*Jawohl!*" (Yes!) answers the defendant quickly to the ritual question. The trial has officially started.

Standing for more than one hour, locked up in his glass booth in front of the judges of the Israeli court, Adolf Eichmann listened to the indictment that in fifteen different counts spelled out the details of his crimes in cold bureaucratic language. Eichmann went from standing rigidly at attention, as would appear customary for an SS officer, to a more relaxed attitude with his head tilted slightly to the right. While Judge Landau enumerates the now sadly familiar names of the death camps, Eichmann keeps on biting his lower lip in an attempt to hide his nervousness behind a mask of indifference. However, his quick glances at his defense lawyer Servatius, the slight twist that distorts his lips, and everything in his body language betrays an inner tension that he tries to break from time to time by blowing his nose into a large white handkerchief that he extracts from the inside pocket of his jacket.

The first count of the indictment accuses Eichmann of having been the cause, during the years 1939–1945, of the death of millions of Jews in his capacity as the official responsible for the so-called "final solution" to the Jewish problem. The defendant, along with others, caused the death of the Jews in the extermination camps of Auschwitz, Chelmno, Belzec, Sobibor, Treblinka, and Maidanek. Immediately following the occupation of Poland in 1939 the defendant sent in special action groups of SS, known as *Einsatzgruppen*, dedicated to the extermination of the Jews. He organized mass deportations of Jews from the following countries: Germany, Austria, Italy, Bulgaria, Belgium, Hungary, the Soviet Union, the Baltic States, Denmark, Holland, Yugoslavia, Greece, Luxembourg, Monaco, Norway, Poland, Czechoslovakia, France, and Romania.

The second count of the indictment deals with the living conditions imposed upon millions of Jews in order to bring about their death. In the third count are listed the measures taken against the Jews within occupied Europe, depriving them of their rights as human beings, oppressing them, and subjecting them to unspeakable torture.

The fourth count accuses the defendant of having issued orders to prevent childbirth among the Jews.

After these crimes against the Jewish people, the indictment lists the crimes committed against humanity. As spelled out in the fifth, sixth, and seventh counts, the defendant brought about the massacre of the civilian Jewish population; he persecuted the Jews for religious and racial reasons; and organized the systematic confiscation of their possessions.

The other crimes against humanity that Eichmann was being accused of included the deportation of half a million Polish civilians from 1940 to 1942 (count IX); the deportation of fourteen thousand Slovenes (count X); and thousands of gypsies (count XI), as well as one hundred Czechoslovak children from the village of Lidice (count XII). The indictment ends with the defendant's participation in criminal organizations like the SS (XIII), the SD (XIV), and the Gestapo—the Nazi secret police (XV).

At the end of the reading Eichmann answered with a *Jawohl!* for the third time that day when the judge asked whether the indictment was clear to him. Then defense attorney Servatius responded.

Robert Servatius is a lawyer from Cologne who was selected by one of Eichmann's brothers residing in Linz, Austria, to take on Adolf's defense. With his happy round face and small blue eyes behind his glasses he looks like a typical German tourist and we can only see his fat bull neck sticking out of his black robe. After having accepted to act as defense lawyer he threatened to withdraw because of a lack of funds and the Israeli government had to guarantee that it would pay him $20,000 for his services. He undoubtedly has a difficult task but in his contacts with the Israeli press corps he displayed some rather bad taste and made a negative impression. He brought a blonde secretary with him who sits at the far left of the long table this morning and a young German lawyer to help him, Dieter Wechtenbruch, who is under thirty and sits to his left.

Servatius has based his defense strategy on a few procedural disputes and even though this was already known as of yesterday, due to the depth and quantity of his objections having to do with fundamental issues, it still caused some amazement.

The first objection coming from the defense concerns the entire Court. He stated that Jewish judges couldn't possibly be objective because they would harbor prejudices due to personal feelings given the fact that the entire Jewish nation was harmed by the massacre.

Therefore the only solution would be a neutral or international tribunal.

Eichmann's defense attorney then went on to attack the law being used to place the defendant on trial: the Israeli law on Nazi crimes. "Such a law" he said "is contrary to the rights of individuals since it seeks to punish actions taking place outside Israeli territory before the creation of the State of Israel against persons who were not Israeli nationals at the time they became victims."

Another objection is that the defendant is being brought to trial after having been kidnapped in Argentina on orders emanating from the State of Israel; and in order to prove that the order came from the State, Servatius asks that Zvi Tohar and Gad Shimoni be called as witnesses since they were both employees of the Israeli national airline El Al.

"The defendant cannot be held accountable for the actions of the State," said Servatius. "The State ordered certain actions and can only be held accountable for them. Such moral responsibility has been accepted by the Federal Republic of Germany in Bonn that agreed to make reparation as a form of expiation."

Servatius has finished; he spoke for a little over one hour, seeking to be brief after having stated his legal arguments in writing, without any rhetorical flourish and having to interrupt his flow after each sentence to allow for translation into Hebrew. He was reading a text that he had carefully prepared together with the Israeli counselor that the bar association had placed at his disposal as evidenced by the judgment citations of the Israeli High Court of Justice.

Now Public Prosecutor Gideon Hausner rises to respond to the objections. Rather short and frail, with a receding hairline, and wearing a pair of thick eyeglasses, more erudite than brilliant, Hausner has none of the expected traits of the great prosecutor. Only an empty chair separates him from his adversary, as he dispassionately rejected the arguments presented by the defense attorney.

"The issue of Adolf Eichmann's arrest and transfer to Israel has already been debated by the Security Council that noted that Eichmann would appear before this Court. On the other hand no one requested his extradition to place him on trial and there is therefore no conflict between the State of Israel and any other State on this matter."

"As for the argument that the Jews since they are victims cannot pass judgment on Eichmann at this time, I shall recall the opinion of Professor Goodhart when the Nuremberg Tribunal was set up by judges of the victorious nations. No one can remain neutral when faced with the crime of genocide and if such a judge did in fact exist he should be precisely the one that must recuse himself. To disqualify all Jewish judges because of who they are is unacceptable since if they do feel the pain in their flesh it is also certain that they shall base their judgment solely on the evidence that shall be introduced here."

Hausner then quoted at length the legal precedents of the British and American legal systems of the last one hundred years that are used in Israel to show how the circumstances in which the defendant is brought to justice do not influence the judgment itself, assuming he has had a fair trial. "I would like to recall the Pettibone case tried by the Idaho Supreme Court on March 16, 1906..."

Hausner's words are drowned out by laughter from the public that obviously couldn't understand certain fine legal points.

Judge Landau gets angry: "I shall expel from the courtroom anyone who laughs!" It's the first time Landau raises his voice and for a brief moment he loses his benevolent smile.

Wednesday April 12

Hausner continued all day with his refutation of the preliminary objections that Servatius made yesterday. The Chief Prosecutor rejected the objection that the defendant acted on the basis of orders he had received and recalled that the responsibility for the crimes committed relates to individuals as is specified in the Human Rights declaration of the United Nations. The fourth principle of Nuremberg approved by the United Nations General Assembly in 1950 had established the individual responsibility of war criminals. He then denied that reparations may be used as expiation because the Jews will never be able to forget those who killed and massacred them.

As for the law against Nazi crimes, Hausner showed that any such laws must of necessity be retroactive, since no one could have foreseen such crimes in advance. Such a law became necessary to fill a legal void that was created at the end of the war, by applying the principles accepted by all civilized people but that were being discussed and were valid even at the time the crimes were committed.

After quoting Grotius and Amos the prophet, Hausner then recalled the tripartite Moscow declaration of 1943 and the London agreement of 1945 that led to the creation of the Nuremberg Tribunal, saying that they did not start anything new but established that murder remains such even when ordered by the Führer. Similar laws were introduced in seventeen European countries, including Germany. The only new element in Israeli law is to be found in the definition of crimes committed against the Jewish people whom the Nazis had decided to exterminate.

Hausner also spoke at length about the court's right to judge crimes committed outside its national territory. Because of modern communications the territorial principle has lost much of its meaning and cannot be considered as the only principle of international law. He recalled the case of the ship *Lotus* in 1920 when the International Tribunal of The Hague admitted Turkey's right to try French citizens for crimes committed against Turkish citizens beyond Turkish territorial waters. Then, citing Vattel's *The Law of Nations*, Hausner said:

"The rights of peoples have already defined some criminals as *hostes humani generis*, enemies of the human race. They are those who in the Bible have the mark of Cain on their forehead. Just as with the pirates of the sea or the slave merchants, anyone who lays a hand on them may bring them to justice!"

From his glass booth Eichmann followed the course of the debate very carefully. Two agents with red and white shoulder boards are sitting just behind him and like those guarding the inside of the courtroom they are not armed. To Hausner's right today were all the members of the prosecution: Yakov Bar-Or, with his dark beard and black *yarmulke*; the international law expert Jacob Robinson; and Gavriel Bach, the brilliant young man who helped section "06" prepare the preliminary investigation.

Both the pit and the balcony, however, were half empty: the newsmen and the general public have little use for legalistic arguments and the trial could well sink into the boredom of citations. But while this less than dramatic beginning has disappointed parts of public opinion, it remains important because it touches upon issues of international law that have long been up for debate at the United Nations, among them the absence of a Court for genocide and an international penal code.

Lord Russell of Liverpool, the eminent British jurist and the author of *The Scourge of the Swastika,* who acted as the prosecutor in the trials of Nazi war criminals, is also present at the proceedings in order to write a book. "It will be somewhat of a new edition of the now classic book by Reitlinger," he told me. Then he added: "This court is not competent to stand in judgment of Eichmann, but it is the only one in the world able to do so since no other country has requested his extradition. This is the first trial that will be able to shed full light on the Nazi massacres and the anti-Semitic persecutions; among the many volumes of the Nuremberg judgments there were only six pages on the crimes committed against the Jews!"

Thursday, April 13

There will be no hearings today: according to the Jewish calendar it is the commemoration of the Jews who died. At the *Yad Vashem* institute in Jerusalem a great mausoleum has been inaugurated, dedicated to those who died in the concentration camps and called the "Hall of Remembrance."

According to Jewish tradition the tombs of the wise men are covered with tents: that's why the rooftop that can be seen in the shade has the slanted shape of a tent. On the floor there is an eternal flame near the names of the main concentration camps, in order to avoid walking over them the visitor takes a kind of elevated gangplank. Outside the structure rests on uncut basalt that gives the impression of the masses of corpses in the Nazi death camps.

Hundreds of people have congregated this morning to commemorate the day of Remembrance. At 8 a.m. throughout the country sirens were blaring for two minutes—inside the factories, offices, and schools—in memory of those killed by the fury of Adolf Eichmann and his henchmen. Commemorative candles are lit in the homes since yesterday. In a ground floor apartment I saw a woman crying near the burning candles: the trial had reopened old wounds.

Friday, April 14

Today the court will convene for only one session rather than the two usually held on weekdays. The doors will close on the courtroom at 1 p.m. and shall reopen only next Monday; there will be no hearings on Saturdays and Sundays in order to honor both Jewish and Christian holidays and the newsmen will have a long weekend to visit the country and sum up their impressions.

Hausner has at last ended the jumble of legal precedents. Without a doubt he selected this path to place the trial on a solid legal basis from the start in contrast to the multiple Nazi illegal acts that are to be judged here. However, this doesn't change the fact that his arguments remain unintelligible to most people.

"If we were to accept the theory of the state reason," said Hausner, "we would reach the absurd conclusion that in a dictatorship such as Germany's there could only be one defendant, Adolf Hitler. But not even according to German law can an illegal order be used to justify an illegal act. I therefore ask that all the defense's objections be rejected."

"At this point in the trial," answered Servatius, "we must establish whether the court is competent or not. The legal void created after the Second World War was never filled: some United Nations projects remained at the stage of idealistic aspirations. According to international law this court is not competent. One could bring up the thought of vengeance. It was however rejected by the Israeli Minister of Foreign Affairs herself, Mrs. Golda Meir, at the Security Council session at the U.N. on June 12, 1960.

"The idea of expiation could be justified but it does not require a special law nor can the defendant expiate for the actions of an entire nation.

"The chief prosecutor has stated that each country has the right to pass judgment on the enemies of human kind. But I may answer that the defendant no longer represents a threat to humanity. Following the end of the Hitler regime he became a peaceful citizen. He had the misfortune of having to execute the orders of an inhuman regime: but he is now freed from the oath he had to take that constituted the basis for the orders he followed."

The surprising statement coming from Servatius caused a shudder throughout the courtroom: he displays not even a minimum of sensitivity! President Landau delays until Monday the court's decisions on the defense's preliminary objections and adjourns the session.

Monday, April 17

There is a lot of expectation for the prosecutor's reading of the indictment; with the close of the procedural objections the actual trial can now begin. Beyond the metal fence that surrounds *Beit Haam* there are many groups of people. Given the size of the courtroom they have no chance of being able to attend the trial. A shameless spring sunshine fills the sky as the silent bystanders gather together, then break up soon after, following the polite invitation of a policeman. All traffic has been diverted and *Beit Haam* is now eerily silent.

Judge Landau begins the session by reading the court's answer regarding the issue of its own competence. "We must reject the exception made by the defense regarding the objectivity of the judges," he states, "because while the memory of the killings shakes every Jew it is also true that as it is our duty we shall pass judgment based only on the evidence that is accepted here. As for the court's competence it is founded on Israeli law and the way the defendant was brought to justice is of no importance. We must therefore reject the defense's request to introduce Tohar and Shimoni as witnesses as well." Turning to Eichmann Landau then said: "The defendant will rise. You have heard the indictment. Do you accept the first part of the indictment?"

Eichmann answered *Im Sinne der Anklage nicht schuldig.* "According to the indictment I am not guilty." For fifteen times as many as the counts of the indictment, Eichmann repeated the formula that had already been used by other Nazi criminals during the Nuremberg Trials. Following his answering "yes" three times on the first day, these are the first sentences that Eichmann was heard pronouncing in the courtroom.

The indictment, which was to last two days, is divided in various chapters that we shall briefly condense.

"When I stand before you here, judges of Israel, to lead the Prosecution of Adolf Eichmann, I am not standing alone. With me are six million accusers. But they cannot rise to their feet and point an accusing finger towards him who sits in the dock and cry: 'I accuse.' For their ashes are piled up on the hills of Auschwitz and the fields of Treblinka and are strewn in the rivers of Poland. Their graves are scattered throughout the length and breadth of Europe. Their blood cries out but their voice is not heard. Therefore it is my duty to be their spokesman and I will express this tragic indictment in their name.

Introduction

"The history of the Jewish people is filled with tears and pain. But in all of human history there is no other man against whom such an indictment could be addressed. Murder is not something new. But it was only in the 20th century that this new form of murder has made an appearance: carried out not because of a sudden moment of passion, but rather as the result of a premeditated decision and careful planning; and not aimed at a single victim but against an entire people.

"In the course of this trial we shall encounter a new kind of murderer: someone who commits his crime at his desk and only rarely gets his hands dirty. Eichmann planned and organized and ordered that this ocean of blood be spilled using every tool to massacre, steal, and torture. He is therefore as responsible as if he had personally thrown millions of Jews into the ditch.

"Many trials took place after the Second World War to make sure those horrors wouldn't be repeated. But the tragedy of the Jews was never at the center of the proceedings in those trials. It was one among several other counts under consideration but never the main one.

Adolf Eichmann, on the other hand, was the only one to be exclusively in charge of the Jews and to handle their extermination.

"We ask how all this could be possible? It will be the task of historians and sociologists to uncover the root causes of this evil. We shall attempt here to explain briefly something that human reasoning cannot explain.

"Nazism was certainly the product of several circumstances coming together at the same time. Germany's defeat, the ensuing economic problems, and the futile divisions of the political parties. But Hitler remained in power because the people were ready to accept him as their leader. In his book, *Mein Kampf,* which serves as a blueprint, he had written: "Every manifestation of human culture is almost exclusively the product of Aryan creative power. The Aryan alone represents the archetype of the term MAN."

"Racial purity became the foundation of the Nazi program. Only Aryans were qualified to be citizens, which was the reason behind the Nuremberg Laws. The concept of "Subhuman"—*Untermensh*—was created to define all those who were not Aryan. Hitler didn't create anti-Semitism. Its roots are to be found in ignorance and prejudice, superstition and envy. But the Nazis turned anti-Semitism into a doctrine of hatred that would inevitably lead to Auschwitz.

"The Jews were accused of being at the same time communists and capitalists; weak and defenseless, they represented an easy target for National Socialist propaganda. Eichmann himself stated that "the Jewish Question was a useful tactic to divert attention from military defeats… Every time there were problems we would go back to the Jewish Question, thus immediately creating a diversion."

"To give a complete picture we must say that in Germany there were thousands of scientists and members of the clergy who dared to help the Jews, but they remained a tiny minority. The overwhelming majority of the German people accepted the new regime and witnessed the most serious crime ever committed in human history.

"In order to humiliate the Jews they sought to eliminate the Bible and even to "redeem" Jesus from his Jewish origins. The notorious forgery, *The Protocols of the Elders of Zion,* about the "Jewish conspiracy to rule the world," was brought back and widely distributed. The accusations of ritual crimes was also renewed. Anti-Semitism became an export item toward the fascist parties in occupied countries; anti-Semitism was a weapon at the hands of the Nazis. Germany has been defeated but anti-Semitism lives on and sometimes it wakes up again and draws swastikas on the walls at night.

"The wicked never repent even on the threshold of hell," says the old Jewish proverb. As Hitler wrote in his political testament a few hours before his death in 1945: "…and above all I order all Germans to fight without pity against international Jewry." Even at the time of his death Hitler tried to foment hatred for the destruction of the Jewish people.

The SS, SD, and Gestapo

"Various official entities of the Reich were used to carry out the persecution of the Jews, including the Foreign Ministry, the Propaganda Ministry, and the army. However, the main instruments were three criminal organizations: the SS, the SD, and the Gestapo. Eichmann was a member of all three organizations.

"The SS (*Schutzstaffel*) was created in 1925 as the elite troops of the SA, the storm troopers of the Nazi Party founded in 1921. Heinrich Himmler was appointed *Reichsführer SS,* or the head of the SS and later on he created the *Waffen SS* as elite military units that were to police the regular army. The SS therefore became a powerful organization with their own army, separate stores of weapons and munitions and even separate laws and regulations.

"The SD (*Sicherheitsdienst der Reichführers SS*) was an internal organization within the party headed by Reinhard Heydrich; its task was to collect all possible information on party members and opponents to the regime, including their private lives.

"In 1936 Himmler became the supreme leader of the criminal and political police. Following the outbreak of the Second World War he divided the SS into a dozen sections, one of them being the RSHA (*Reichssicherheifshauptant*), the Reich Main Security Office headed by Heydrich, had the mission to suppress any form of opposition to the regime. Department ("*Amt*") IV was the Gestapo under Heinrich

Müller and it included Section IV B-4, the Jewish section headed by Eichmann.

"The SS organized the concentration camps, the work and death camps, and were named a criminal organization by the Nuremberg Tribunal. The extermination camps used every modern technique and Rudolf Höss, the commandant at Auschwitz, was able to have a quiet family life while on the opposite side of the electrified fence five to ten thousand people were being killed every day…

"Every form of humiliation was deliberately used to break down the self-confidence of the prisoners. The Nazis knew how to exploit every bodily need and human weakness for their own ends.

"After each dragnet they would purposefully spread the rumor that no such actions would be repeated and that the survivors would not be arrested.

"It is extraordinary that even in that hell there were Jews who managed to keep true to the divine image and refused to bend. Others collaborated and followed orders as *Kapos,* or as members of the Councils of Elders. But this trial does not concern them since this is not the trial of the victims but rather of the jailers.

"We shall not discuss the path that Jewish leaders should have followed inside the jaws of the tiger—that dispute has no place in these proceedings. I don't think we can now establish a set rule according to which the victims were to act in their relations with the beast; namely, whether they should have attempted to save whatever they could or incite the community to revolt. We are all naturally proud of the uprising of the Warsaw Ghetto and the partisan resistance, but such issues must be left to historians. In this instance it is Adolf Eichmann who is on trial.

The Defendant

"Adolf Eichmann was born in Solingen, Germany, on March 19, 1906, and moved to Austria as a child. He joined the Nazi party and the SS in 1932 after being introduced by his friend Ernst Kaltenbrunner, who would later become head of the RSHA. One year later he went back to Germany and in 1934 took a special course at the

Dachau camp that was set up as a school of violence for aspiring SS leaders. The following year he joined the Jewish section of the SD and was involved exclusively in collecting information. To this end he was sent on a short mission to the Middle East.

"With the conquest of Austria Eichmann was stationed in Vienna to organize the forced emigration of the Jews. This was his first assignment and he handled it with great diligence. Within a few hours at the Center for Emigration the Jews were deprived of their citizenship, their possessions, their jobs, and given a safe conduct allowing them to leave Austria within a given period, never to return. The system was so efficient that it was copied by other cities in the Reich.

"In September 1939 Himmler merged the Security Police (SIPO-*Sicherheits polizei*) and the party's information service (SD), and Eichmann was called to Berlin to manage the central office for Jewish emigration.

"In his contacts with Jewish leaders Eichmann was often duplicitous and hypocritical, aggressive and understanding at the same time. In the meantime his success in persecuting the Jews provided him with his initial promotions.

"At the end of 1939, because of his experience, he was put in charge of the deportation of the Jews from occupied Poland into the Nisko region. He became head of RSHA Section IV B4.

"In the occupied countries he would send his personal representatives to the local police command or the German embassies in the satellite countries. In the end Eichmann himself, as the greatest expert in extermination, was sent to Hungary to carry out in the shortest possible time his mission of death.

"Eichmann was responsible for the ghettos and the death camps and he held a unique position in the RSHA: he could go directly to Himmler and by-pass his immediate supervisors. His responsibility placed him in contact with the highest authorities of the Foreign Ministry and other Reich ministries, with heads of government in occupied countries and military commanders. It should therefore come as no surprise that with regard to Jewish issues he would hand out orders to those of higher rank than himself.

"In October 1941 he was promoted to Lieutenant colonel of the SS (*Obersturmbannführer*) with an evaluation that stated, among other things: "Eichmann has already performed exceptionally well in the work of eliminating the Jews of Austria. Thanks to his work some important properties were added to the Reich. Eichmann is now working on important problems of evacuation and transfer of population. Given the importance of that task his promotion is to be considered to be in the interest of the Service." In December 1944 he became the head of Section IV A4, which handled Jewish issues and political problems with the churches.

"Eichmann will tell you that he followed his supervisor's orders but this doesn't make for a legal or moral defense, as it has been previously established at Nuremberg.

"We shall prove to the court that he went beyond the orders he was given and was responsible for massacres that hadn't been decided by his superiors. Even in October 1944, when Himmler issued the order to interrupt deportations from Hungary, Eichmann organized an infamous "forced march" that turned into a death march.

"He displayed his personal initiative also by stopping any attempt to escape of any single Jew, even when the authorities were ready to make exceptions.

"Just before being hanged, Rudolf Höss, the Auschwitz commandant, described Eichmann as follows: "Eichmann was extremely devoted to his mission and was convinced that the extermination of the Jews was necessary in order to save Germany. He was adamantly opposed to any kind of attempt to make a selection of those Jews who could work; he thought this constituted a permanent threat to his plans for the 'final solution,' since that would have allowed for some Jews to stay alive."

"Wisliceny, another colleague of Eichmann's, described him in the death cell at Bratislava prison: "Based on my personal experience I can say that even though Eichmann was covered by orders he had received from Hitler and Himmler, played a determining role in the extermination of the Jews in Europe and must be held fully responsible since there were other ways around Hitler's orders."

"Eichmann was fully aware of his actions and even after the collapse of the Nazi monster, he chose to remain loyal to his ideas. He did not repent and remains convinced to this day that it was correct to kill millions of people.

The "Final Solution" of the Jewish Problem

"The Nazi program to exterminate the Jews and the methods used to carry it out changed as the circumstances warranted and various phases became readily apparent. At first, while the Nazis still worried about the reaction of international public opinion, the preferred solution was forced emigration. But once they realized that the world was just watching without saying anything and the circumstances were favorable, they decided to move on to total extermination. There was a transition between the two phases when the Nazis pretended to consider a territorial solution to the Jewish problem.

"The defendant took an active part in the programming of all these projects and was responsible for their implementation.

"The night between November 9 and 10, 1938, became known as 'the night of broken glass' (*Kristallnacht*). During that night of terror the Nazis broke into Jewish homes to destroy and to rob. Hundreds synagogues were burned, thousands of people were sent to concentration camps 'to protect them from public fury.' Nazi Germany brought back to Europe the burning of synagogues—something that had not been seen since the darkest days of the Middle Ages.

"The Nazi leaders concluded that since all this could take place without provoking world reaction the time had come to move on to the 'final solution.'

"But in 1939 they continued with forced emigration from Germany, Austria, and Czechoslovakia once they had been occupied. Both results—the physical elimination of the Jews through emigration and later through murder and the theft of their possessions—were almost closely connected.

"In his January 30, 1939, speech to the Reichstag Hitler said, among other things: 'If the Jews who are in control of world capitalism will again lead us into a world war, the result will not be the spread of

Bolshevism and the victory of Judaism but rather the extermination of European Jewry.'

"Adolf Hitler kept only one of his promises: that one that has brought eternal shame on Germany. And to carry it out he used the services of another Adolf, Adolf Eichmann, who is here, facing you now.

"In June 1940 Heydrich, head of the main security office, informed Foreign Minister von Ribbentrop that emigration no longer represented a practical solution to the Jewish problem. At that point a plan to deport all Jews to Madagascar at a rate of one million per year was being considered, but was never implemented. Another attempt at territorial concentration of the Jews was in the Village of Nisko in the Lublin region of Poland, where Eichmann deported Jews from Vienna, Bohemia, and Moravia during the winter of 1939.

"The attack on the Soviet Union on June 22, 1941, and the entry of the United States into the war on the side of the Allies, signaled a decisive change in the plans for extermination. On July 31, 1941, Göring gave Heydrich the following instructions: "I give you the order to make all the necessary preparations, both practical and organizational, toward a comprehensive solution of the Jewish problem within the German sphere of influence in Europe. I also order you to provide me with a general plan regarding the implementation of the desired "final solution" (*Endlösung*) of the Jewish problem."

"In the course of that summer Eichmann went to Auschwitz to select a location for the extermination facilities and discuss technical details with Rudolf Höss. In October 1941 Himmler issued an order banning Jewish emigration from the territories of the Reich. The initial plans had been set and the methods to be used agreed upon: rather than expelling the Jews they were to be killed. That same month a functionary of the ministry for occupied territories wrote that an agreement had been reached with Eichmann to use gas chambers as a solution to the Jewish problem.

"In order to resolve the various problems Eichmann proposed a gathering of the civil servants of the various ministries, involved which Heydrich approved. Eichmann was in charge of preparing the conference that took place on January 20, 1942, at Wannsee, a Berlin suburb. The directors general of the various ministries took part and Heydrich gave the main address. He recalled the "practical experiments" that had already taken place in the East, which provided useful feedback. (He was referring to the recent massacres in occupied Russia.) Heydrich then announced that following Himmler's orders emigration was to end and the evacuation of the Jews to the East would begin to implement the "final solution." We shall prove that this term meant the killing of the Jews. In the occupied territories the officers of the Security Police had to work in coordination with the German embassies. We shall prove that Eichmann was the officer responsible at the RSHA and that the term 'special treatment' meant murder. That conference also discussed the children of mixed marriages and how, in specific cases, they would be allowed to remain in Germany on condition that they agree to being sterilized.

"Adolf Eichmann therefore had reached a position of enormous authority, allowing him to issue orders regarding the destruction of the Jewish people. Every aspect of the extermination process concerned him directly. To replace the shootings that, according to him, would have turned the executioners into sadists, the more 'elegant' system of the gas chambers was chosen.

"Eichmann was the central authority for Jewish matters and the foreign ministry turned to him when it wished to keep a few thousand foreign Jews alive to be able to exchange them for German citizens. He was particularly careful to avoid any emigration to Palestine because of his commitments to the Mufti of Jerusalem.

"When the Argentine government requested news of its citizen Gerson Wollner, who was living in Poland, and the Foreign Ministry asked Himmler that he should not be sent to a concentration camp, Eichmann's cynical answer was that the Jew in question had died of a heart attack in spite of the excellent treatment given to him.

"In the course of this trial we will prove with what care and diligence Eichmann managed to close every small loophole through which even a single Jew could possibly escape. We shall see how he dealt with German diplomats and everyone in the occupied territories who failed to fully collaborate. We shall witness his anger toward Italian officials who on many occasions managed to thwart his plans; his fury against

Denmark, which in one brave operation successfully transferred all of its Jews into Sweden. When the Jews in Rome had been arrested 'practically under the windows of the Vatican' (according to the words of a German diplomat), the German authorities were asked to leave the Italian Jews in the work camps rather than deport them, but the request was rejected and the Jews were sent to Auschwitz.

"Many millions perished in the Second World War. But the extermination of the Jews was not connected to any military action. It cannot be compared to the bombing of cities or the submarine war, since they were acts of war and it is not for us to decide whether they were legitimate or not. However, the massacre of the Jews was not motivated by any military considerations. While the German army was in desperate need of all means of transportation that had become extremely scarce, trains and engines were assigned to deport the Jews to the death camps. And even though men were needed at the front, those required to carry out the massacres were always available.

"The extermination program was to be kept absolutely secret. First of all, to fool the victims themselves, thereby facilitating the transportation. Second, to hide what was going on from the rest of the world. The words used were to be "transfers for forced labor" rather than mentioning deportations. But the secret couldn't be kept very long. The thousands of special brigades (*Einsatzgruppen*), soldiers, the employees of the register office, the mailmen, the thousands of soldiers on leave—all knew as well, so that in the end one may say that millions of Germans knew that the massacres were taking place.

"We shall now examine Eichmann's bloody actions within the various countries."

The prosecutor underscored the persecutions in Poland, the Soviet Union, Western Europe, the central and southern parts, Hungary, and inside the extermination camps. To avoid any repetition the summary of these sections of the indictment shall be placed ahead of the hearings as they relate to various countries. This will be the only exception we have allowed in the strict chronological account of the trial. We now offer a summary of two final chapters of the indictment that lasted two consecutive days.

A Lost World

Tuesday, April 18

"The Jewish people were deprived of many millions of its children, at least six million. But this represents more than one-third of the total Jewish population: this means the destruction of communities that made up the most vital elements from the point of view of national consciousness, creative force, cultural and spiritual resources, and devotion to Jewish values. A national community was exterminated that had been an integral part of Europe since the Second Century B.C. and that had given Nobel Prize winners and geniuses in all areas of science and the arts—Albert Einstein, Sigmund Freud, Ernst Chain, Martin Buber, Stefan Zweig, Franz Kafka, Marc Chagall, Bronislaw Huberman, and Arthur Rubinstein.

"The Jewish villages of Eastern Europe, the shelter where thousands of Jews were living and where family traditions were kept alive, that was a center of Bible studies, were erased from the face of the earth. An entire civilization had been destroyed. But thanks to Providence Eichmann's plans were thwarted and couldn't be completed."

The Charges and the Proof

"We shall prove the guilt of the accused as the planner, initiator, organizer and executor of the so-called 'final solution' of the Jewish problem as well as his direct participation in this criminal project. We shall prove that the accused carried out these crimes with the publicized intent of destroying the Jewish people. We shall prove that his actions were a crime against the Jewish people and against humanity and were war crimes.

"As proof we shall show the court documents and introduce witnesses. The killing of millions of Jews also means the elimination of as many million witnesses; but there are survivors who have the ability to describe what they saw with their own eyes and suffered on their bodies.

"I still fear that once all the material we have in our possession has been introduced we shall still only offer a faint idea of the enormous human and national tragedy that hit this generation of Jews.

"Adolf Eichmann shall enjoy a privilege that he never gave to any of his victims. He shall be able to defend himself in court. His fate shall be decided on the basis of the law and the evidence that the prosecution is under the obligation to introduce.

"And the judges of Israel shall issue a sentence dictated by truth and justice."

Hausner's argument, which lasted some ten hours, had come to an end. It was without a doubt his masterpiece: a kind of "quick survey" of anti-Semitism that has not been surpassed until now and that deserves to be placed in every text in the world. His voice, strident at times, never sounded rhetorical or melodramatic; on the contrary, it remained cold as is best suited for historical description. But when he went beyond the general picture and lingered on a detail, such as a poem, every one of us journalists and the audience were swept up by emotion. This is probably the best feature of the indictment offered by the prosecutor: to have provided a human face to the dry numbers of those killed.

Hausner must also share the credit with the investigators of section "06" of the police force that prepared the inquiry. Searching in the archives of the German foreign ministry, the Poliakov documentation center in Paris, the Yad Vashem historical institute in Jerusalem, and hundreds of other sources, they performed some excellent teamwork, like the editors of a sad encyclopedia of the massacre.

The task of the prosecution that must prove Eichmann's personal responsibility was far from simple, since Eichmann was always careful to make sure that any trace had been erased, appearing as little as possible in any official photographs, and not signing office correspondence.

Hausner may perhaps be criticized because in his quest to prove the brutality of the accused he may have exonerated other notorious international fascists. No doubt they were less cruel than Eichmann. However, Ferenc Szálasi in Hungary, Father Joseph Tiso in Slovakia,

Philippe Pétain and Pierre Laval in France—all had many murders on their conscience. Hausner also recalled that the Republic of Salò was scolded by Eichmann's office because its foreign ministry requested information regarding the Jew Bernard Taubert. But this can in no way change the fact the Salò government effectively helped its Nazi comrades in arms. On October 16, 1943, in Rome, the SS was deporting the Jews with the assistance of some Italian units, like the PAI,[16] the Decima Mas, the Black Brigades, the gangs of the Palazzo Braschi and the Via Tasso—just to name a few. They did all they could to live up to the Nazi's expectations where Jews and partisans were concerned. However, and in spite of the Fascist Republican government, the overwhelming majority of the Italian people always extended fraternal help to the Jews, often at tremendous personal risk. In the afternoon the witnesses for the prosecution began to appear.

Police inspector Bar-Shalom described how he was able to verify the authenticity of the documents offered by the prosecution. This was a purely technical and uninteresting testimony but it was required to offer a solid basis to the evidence introduced by the prosecutor.

Wednesday, April 19

"Should I begin with France? How did things start in France? Or else how did it take place in Holland? And who initiated things in Holland? Or in the Aegean: I am completely in the dark there…" This is a passage of the Eichmann examination before trial that Inspector Abner Less read to the judges this morning. It was recorded entirely on tape and transcribed on 3,564 typed pages, all of them corrected and signed by the defendant. Inspector Less spoke with Eichmann daily for ten months in his padded cell in the jail that had remained secret until a few days ago. Perhaps no one in the world knows Eichmann as well as he does now, and no one could possibly be better at forecasting his answers and any reaction, however minimal.

Eichmann's voice, just as it was recorded in prison, can be heard from one of the two tape recorders on the prosecution's table; it has a metallic quality that we didn't hear so far from the few words the

16. Polizia dell'Africa Italiana.

defendant had to say in court. It is a voice that seems to come from the dead and Eichmann takes off his earphones to hear it better.

"In June or July at the beginning of the war, Heydrich summoned me and told me that the Führer had ordered the physical extermination of the Jews. At first I didn't grasp the meaning of those carefully chosen words. Then I understood and didn't answer. I had nothing to say about this brutal solution: I had never considered it."

From excerpts of his testimony Eichmann mostly sounded like a coward. He would have us believe that he was nothing but a mild desk-bound romantic employee. He never was a soldier and in fact was exempt from serving at the front. Once in a while we are inclined to believe him. Inspection tours? Yes, he did take many, but only to report back to Müller his superior and he tried to arrive once the operations were completed.

"When I went to see Globocnik in Lublin," the tape recorder goes on rasping, "I noticed a shack. I was told that it was hermetically sealed to kill the Jews, using the exhaust fumes of a submarine engine. It was awful. I am the type of person that can't look at a bleeding wound. I belong to those people who are unable to become doctors. In Chelmno they had the Jews enter a bus naked, but I couldn't watch, and only heard them screaming. Then when I followed the bus I witnessed the most awful thing I saw in my life: the doors were opened and the bodies dumped into a ditch like animals. I also saw teeth being ripped off the corpses. I didn't want to watch and returned to my car."

When he saw some Jews being shot by firing squad in Minsk on the edge of a mass grave where a woman with her hands tied behind her back was still moving, the gentle Eichmann "felt his knees giving in" and fled the scene. But along the way his secret soul was comforted by memories of Francis Joseph awakened by the Lwow railroad station, "a period that I am very much attached to."

His main concern was of an educational nature. "We are teaching our youth to become sadists," he told Müller. "Then they will turn into criminals." This was the reason why the mass shootings could not be the solution. In order to avoid harming his dear SS youth, to avoid seeing "a jet of blood squirting up from the earth like a geyser," Eichmann was compelled to invent something more elegant and more scientific. The secret of the gas chambers was contained in those remarks.

He was unable to answer certain questions that Inspector Less was asking. He claims not to remember too well. The same man who was able to describe to perfection the autumn leaves falling in 1939 or the color of a railroad station was unable to recall the killings.

"I had to inspect the facilities at Auschwitz. There were huge buildings with chimneys that looked like factories. Höss told me each one could hold ten thousand people a day. He even showed me one of those round canisters they were using to kill people. But I didn't want to watch how they gassed the Jews because I would have fainted.

"But the most awful thing I witnessed was at Treblinka. A long line of naked Jews was crossing a bridge toward a large building to be gassed. They were being killed there by *Ziankali...* I think or an acid whose name I can't remember..." Once more Eichmann's perfect memory suddenly fails him! "I didn't know who gave those orders. Personally I never saw a written order to that effect."

Eichmann sent out the invitations to the famous Wannsee Conference that took place in a Berlin suburb in 1942 with top functionaries in attendance. "Heydrich wanted to show that his power had increased and that he had now become the boss of all the Jews. It was the first time I was taking part in a meeting with high-ranking officials and secretaries of state," he said, "and I noticed how it all took place in a very friendly and polite atmosphere. Then cognac was served and the meeting ended. Of that crucial meeting Eichmann today can only recall the cognac. He is clearly deprived of moral sense but if he stopped pretending to be dumb he should be capable of offering a political opinion. Even now what impresses him more than anything is the presence of high-ranking officials. The craving to feel important and advance his career at any cost was the motivation for Eichmann to embark upon his sad journey.

"In the course of the final days of the battle of Berlin I told my men that all was lost, but that according to my estimation the war had claimed the lives of five million Jews. I added that I was ready to leap into the ditch. I would have preferred a bullet rather than to use false documents." But this didn't stop Eichmann the hero from living for fifteen more years using forged documents.

As a final touch to Eichmann's portrait comes this sensational statement: "I had been accustomed to unconditional obedience ever since I was a child. I can't say that my hands are clean. But I was only a subordinate and was never involved in planning. I am ready to pay the price and I know that I can be condemned to death. I do not ask for pity because I don't deserve it. Perhaps I should hang myself publicly for all the anti-Semites to understand the nature of those events. Perhaps I should write a book that will serve as a warning to young people the world over so they will not act this way. Then my task on this earth shall be fulfilled."

According to his self-portrait Eichmann was never a soldier. But the real surprise is that he has the soul of a moralist writer!

The session ends with Eichmann's estimate of the number of victims. Even though he can't give an exact figure, he feels those killed were six million.

At ten the president interrupted the proceedings to observe two minutes of silence in memory of the Israeli dead during the war of independence in 1948. Tomorrow will be the thirteenth anniversary of the State of Israel. What a difference between those who died in combat and those killed in the Nazi ditches!

Thursday, April 20

Today is independence day and thirteen years in the life of this young state. From his cell Eichmann could hear and even perhaps see the *Centurion* tanks, the armored and motorized vehicles, the men and women soldiers marching past, singing in a great military parade. Maybe the fireworks last night, the singing in the streets where people were dancing late into the night, the rumble of the engines this morning made him think about the irony of his fate. After spending most of his life destroying the Jewish people Eichmann can now see it more alive than ever before, so different from those who were taken to the death camps without any possibility of defending themselves. An Italian colleague, Angelo del Bocca, told me: "Perhaps the worse punishment would be to bring him here this morning to watch the parade."

Friday, April 21

This morning we resumed, listening to Eichmann's deposition. Inspector Less asks him: "Going back to the Wannsee Conference, why would you even be invited if you were of such low rank?" Eichmann answered slavishly: "But Mr. Inspector, I was only supposed to send out the invitations and provide Heydrich with some numbers. I could not speak, since I was such a low-level official."

Less: "As for the trains carrying the deportees, did you have orders to use firearms in case someone attempted to escape?"

Eichmann: "I wouldn't know… Of course there were attempts made to flee but had they used their weapons the consequences would have been disastrous. Therefore, I don't think there were any such orders."

Less: "But your department wasn't only dealing with transport issues"

Eichmann: "Yes, in a way that's true. You see, before it could begin the deportation IV B4 had to get everything ready. It wasn't possible for just any official entity to go down the street and arrest the Jews; that was not possible. But IV B4 never received orders to exterminate; it was only supposed to organize the transports."

Less: "Was the final solution of the Jewish problem a law of the Reich?"

Eichmann: "No, but it was an order by the Führer and according to the legal framework of the time it was the law."

In his booth Eichmann listens to himself attentively and keeps on taking notes. This morning a photographer was denied his authorization by President Landau because he had managed to take close-ups of some of the notes. During Hausner's indictment Eichmann had written: "Foolishness… This doesn't concern me, but Heydrich."

Less: "You state that you did not take part in the massacres. But the transports you set up were taking people to the slaughter!"

Eichmann: "Yes, that's true Mr. Inspector. But my orders were to deport people and not everyone who was deported was killed. Otherwise after the war you would not have found 2,400,000 Jews alive."

Less: "That was certainly not thanks to you but because the Allies won the war. In any case you were involved in the extermination plans."

Eichmann: "Yes, I believe I am guilty as an accomplice. I am guilty through my work and my cooperation in the plans. This is clear. Legally I am guilty of complicity."

Less: "We are not discussing the legal aspects but the facts. And you go on saying that this was not your area of responsibility and that you only followed orders."

Eichmann: "Yes I had to do it as head of the IV B4. I had no authority beyond the strict limits of my department."

Less: "There is the photocopy of a document…"

Eichmann: "Yes, it's a telegram from [Edmund] Veesenmayer at the Ministry of Foreign Affairs. He writes, among other things: 'It was agreed with Eichmann that the deportation of the Jews from Budapest was to take place through a very quick surprise action; so that those Jews who were about to emigrate would be deported before they could obtain the necessary documents.' This proves, Mr. Inspector, that not just the security police but also other authorities were putting on pressure for a quick solution. But there was no need for such requests since the pace in Hungary set by Secretary of State [László] Endre was so tight that in Auschwitz they could not receive all the trains…"

Less: "But here it says that they discussed the matter with Eichmann!"

Eichmann: "Yes, but it is of no importance to analyze the thing and establish if there was an agreement among us or not. The pace was set by [László] Baky, no rather by Endre…"

Eichmann gives his personal interpretation to every document shown to him. On other occasions he hides behind the easy excuse of not remembering. In other parts of the recording Eichmann admits to having deported gypsies but didn't know whether they had been sent to Auschwitz to be gassed. He then remembers having questioned the young Hershel Grynszpan in 1943 or 1944, but again he doesn't know what happened to him.

Less reads the notes that he (Eichmann) wrote in the margins of a book where he calls his former colleague Dieter Wisliceny swine, along with Gerhardt Boldt, author of the book in question (*The Last Days of the Reich*).

Eichmann: "Yes. As I was reading I was overtaken by a furious anger and took notes that I felt were of some importance at the time. I wrote that an officer must be true to his oath which is not new at all. That is Kant's imperative, which became the cornerstone of my life."

Moving on to another subject, Less asked him: "Did you believe that the extermination of the Jewish people was essential to the German people?"

Eichmann: "Inspector, had they told me at the time: your father is a traitor, kill him, I would not have hesitated in any way. I blindly obeyed my orders and was completely satisfied with that. I would have carried out any task given to me, blindly and with enthusiasm."

The session ends with that statement, which, as few others, explains the kind of man Eichmann is.

Monday, April 24

Today's hearing was almost entirely dedicated to the testimony of Professor Salo Baron, a scholar of Jewish history at Columbia University in New York. Just before, Inspector Less had testified and answered the questions of defense attorney Servatius, who during cross-examination had asked whether he, Less, had pressured the defendant during his pre-trial examination. The defense is attempting to reduce the value of Eichmann's testimony that the prosecution is turning into an efficient weapon against the defendant.

Professor Baron, like the other witnesses, is wearing a black *yarmulke*, he places his right hand on the Bible, is sworn in, and begins with a description of the condition of the Jewish people on the eve of the Nazi massacres.

He goes into some detail on the statistics of the European Jews who in the 1930s numbered about ten million. The Jews played a key role in the European economy for many centuries, not only as bankers and merchants, but also as industrialists and professionals. After the First World War the Jews had obtained equal civil rights practically all over the world. But *Kristallnacht* signaled a radical change and for the first time it was a government that destroyed scores of synagogues by an action unprecedented even in the Middle Ages.

Baron then described the innumerable mutual assistance institutions that the Jews had created, especially in Poland. Jewish culture was supported by 354 daily newspapers and a vast literature in Hebrew, Yiddish, and Ladino. The Jews also made an exceptional contribution to European culture with scientists such as Einstein and Freud, whose influence will be felt for generations. But, the witness added, the most interesting aspect of Jewish history is the pioneering spirit that motivated the Jews for centuries, forced as they were to find new paths to survive in societies where the best positions were already taken.

The Zionist Movement blossomed between the wars, along with the youth movements that set the foundations for the State of Israel.

The Nazi Party added a new ingredient to anti-Semitism. While in the Middle Ages a converted Jew could live a normal life, the Nazis turned anti-Semitism into a biological destiny, allowing no escape. Professor Baron then quoted from the encyclical of Pope Pius XI of 1937, where the Pontiff wrote: "A real religious persecution is taking place in Germany. We know that this is a terrible persecution equal to few in the course of history." If that was true for the Christians, it was even more so for the Jews! The Nazi massacre is the worst that the Jewish people have endured throughout their history—not only because of the number of victims but because of the disappearance of most of the Jewish leaders. Its consequences are felt to this day. As for those killed, it remains difficult to establish precisely, but it could well go beyond six million and perhaps even reach close to seven million.

Baron has finished; now it was Servatius' turn to ask questions. The first one will amply illustrate his bad taste: "Professor Baron," he asks, "you have provided a summary of Jewish history and anti-Semitism during the last two centuries. Could you tell us the reasons for this negative treatment of the Jewish people?"

This was really too much! Such a question implies that a Jew be aware of the "objective" reason why he is hated by other people, and that such a legitimate reason actually exists. Baron answers that anti-Semitism originates in religious beliefs and hatred for those who are different. He then went into a discussion of historical determinism, which he doesn't believe in, and his testimony ends there.

The long historical disquisitions by Baron, who often seemed to be lecturing at a university colloquium, left the audience rather cold and empty. Perhaps Eichmann needed such a lesson and the conclusion one may draw is this: what kind of punishment will be harsh enough for someone who destroyed hundreds of schools, high schools, and seminaries, thousands of newspaper libraries, school records, the best of a culture that wasn't just Jewish but also European?

A trial can certainly not follow the requirements of the press but some journalists are disappointed today. The dramatic tension that had reached its climax during Hausner's indictment was almost completely diluted by Baron's sociological considerations.

Tuesday, April 25

During this morning's hearing the discussion between the prosecution and the defense was about the introduction into the record of a number of documents, including the well-known deposition by Dieter Wisliceny. "I, Dieter Wisliceny, swear and declare the following..." This was how the 1946 deposition by Wisliceny begins, shortly before he was put to death in Bratislava prison. Few people knew Eichmann as well as Wisliceny, who was at first his superior and then his subordinate in section IV B4. Few had expressed as clear and detailed an indictment of the defendant. This was the reason why the defense had so strenuously opposed that posthumous statement from being entered into the record.

Wisliceny recalls that in Berlin in August or July of 1942 Eichmann showed him an order from Himmler written on paper with red margins, which meant immediate action, regarding the "final solution" to the Jewish problem. Eichmann told him that the term "final solution" meant the biological extermination of the Jewish people. "I was impressed by that document that gave Eichmann the power to kill millions of people," wrote Wisliceny. "I said to him: 'I hope our enemies don't treat us the way we treated the Jews.' And he answered: 'Don't be sentimental. The Führer has ordered the extermination of the Jewish race.'"

What Wisliceny wrote about his former colleague is also of great interest. "I feel that Eichmann's personality was a determining and important factor in the extermination of the Jews. He was a coward who was always trying to cover himself and escape responsibility. He would collect notes and documents showing how Himmler and Kaltenbrunner also shared the blame. When it came to the Jews Eichmann was a cynic. He never expressed any human feelings toward them. He was not immoral: he was completely devoid of any form of morality. During our last conversation (in February 1945), speaking of the defeat he told me: 'I will be happy in my grave knowing that I killed five million Jews. It gives me full satisfaction and a feeling of success.'"

In his glass booth Eichmann keeps on tidying the green files he brings from his cell every morning, and marks with red and black pencils quick notes on the margins and sends little notes to his defense attorney through the policeman who is next to him. He is more precise and methodical than ever but he is probably attempting to cover up his inner tension. He attempted to discredit the deposition by saying that Wisliceny wrote it to try and save his own skin.

The witnesses for the prosecution now begin once more and Chief Prosecutor Hausner has his deputy Bar-Or, who is sitting next to him, proceed with the questioning. In his forties, with a thick little beard and a black yarmulke permanently affixed on his head, Bar-Or has had a lot of experience in criminal trials.

The first witness is Shmuel Grynszpan, the father of the boy who killed the German embassy councilor in 1938 in Paris to protest the suffering perpetuated against his parents and his brothers. The Nazis used the murder as an excuse to unleash the infamous *Kristallnacht*. The elder Grynszpan recounted how he was deported out of Germany in October 1938 on a Saturday with 12,000 other Jews. "The SS grabbed the few pieces of luggage we had and once we were close to the Polish border told us to run, using whips to push us forward. We stayed a few days in Poland without any food in a barn. From there I was able to write to my son who was in Paris."

That postcard prompted the young Grynszpan to draw world attention to the Jewish tragedy.

The following witness, Benno Cohn, was the president of the local Zionist organization in Berlin where he also worked as a lawyer prior to the Second World War. He describes the first few years of the Nazi regime, starting with February 27, 1933, when the Reichstag was set on fire and the initial arrests took place. Many people, including many Jews, were arrested for no reason. After some time the family would receive a note saying, more or less: "Your husband died of a heart attack. To receive the urn with his ashes send three and a half marks to cover postage costs." When the first signs were painted on shop windows saying *Jude raus* ("Jews Go Away"), many Jews had trouble believing what they saw, since many were very much assimilated. There was also written, "Wear the yellow star with pride!"

At the same time the Nazis were carrying on the gradual exclusion of the Jews from the country's economy. "Anyone with one parent or grandfather who is Jewish shall be considered a non-Aryan"—as the 1933 law stated. Books written by Jews were burned in the public squares and Jews were forbidden to play musical works by German composers, The 1935 Nuremberg Laws stated that a Jew could not be a citizen of the Reich and the persecution after being economic became political. That year a prayer was written to be read in the Synagogues on *Yom Kippur* (the highest holy day of the Jewish faith, the Day of Atonement): "On this hour as we are in front of God our hearts are full of sorrow. But we shall express it in silence and this silence shall shout louder than words."

"The night of November 9 to 10, 1938, is known as *Kristallnacht*. Thousands of Jewish shops had their windows shattered and the morning after I found that my office had been ransacked. Thousands of Jews were deported to concentration camps. I saw a synagogue burning and a few Jews attempting to save the Torah scrolls. Two hundred and eighty synagogues were set on fire that night all over Germany. I placed a call to Jerusalem to Moshe Shertok of the Jewish

Agency and told him: Forty thousand men are already in concentration camps. Help us. SOS! But the results were minimal because British authorities refused to give out visas to enter Palestine. And it was almost impossible to obtain any visas to other countries.

"At the beginning of 1939 I met Eichmann for the second time. He was in his office wearing civilian clothes. There was an SS officer, probably his commanding officer, who seemed to inhibit him because of his presence. Eichmann began to scream immediately at me and at the other Jewish community leaders who had come with me. He was using particularly vulgar and violent language, words I was hearing for the first time. He was furious because of an article published in France that described him as "a bloodthirsty dog." He kept on threatening to pack us off to a concentration camp. He also mentioned the issue of mass emigration for which he was setting up a central office similar to the one he was in charge of in Vienna that my other friends had visited. Then he threw us out. We knew that war was at hand and that we should do what we could to get the Jews out of Germany and we had no other choice but to collaborate with him."

Benno Cohn's testimony came to an end. The portrait of Eichmann he gave was quite different from that of the meek low level bureaucrat he tries to pass himself off as; at SS headquarters Eichmann was playing "tough." His defense attorney, attempting to salvage whatever he could, asked the witness: "You were all fearful of being arrested. But did Eichmann do anything to you after that meeting?" "No. I don't know of any decision of that kind," Cohn answered and Servatius sat down looking satisfied at this minor tactical success.

The prosecution had asked that the witness read a passage from a book about Jewish history. Judge Benjamin Halevy, looking worried, asked: "If this follows the metaphysical or philosophical discussion of yesterday I feel it is out of place today…"

The afternoon session ends with the testimony by Aharon Lindenstrauss, who was working in the Palestine Office in Berlin. He relates how at the beginning of 1939, before leaving Germany along with other Jewish community leaders from Berlin, he was ordered to go to Vienna without knowing why. In the Austrian capital they went to see Eichmann, who had set up his Central Office for Emigration in the

Rothschild palace. Eichmann was in civilian clothes with a few SS officers and Jewish officials who "stood at attention not daring to utter a word, like obedient soldiers." "Eichmann asked us to line up and told us, using vulgar language, that we should accelerate emigration and set up a Central Office in Berlin similar to the one in Vienna. He also announced a special tax on emigrants. We returned to Berlin thinking that the situation was desperate. At Eichmann's headquarters in Vienna there was an air of organized expulsion."

Wednesday, April 26

This morning the court decided to add the testimony of Wisliceny, given at Bratislava prison in 1946, into the record over the defense's objections. The prosecutor reads a few parts of the document. Wisliceny relates how Eichmann organized the deportations in 1941 and how he used the mass shooting of Soviet commissars that Hitler had ordered to also kill the Jews. "Globocnik was the first to use the gas chambers to kill human beings. As the war went on and a German victory was obviously impossible, Eichmann put on more pressure to complete the deportations and the massacres." According to Rolf Günther, his assistant, and the only person to have any influence upon him, the pace of the deportations never seemed fast enough. Eichmann was successful because of the following:

1. He had the complete confidence of Himmler, Heydrich, Müller, and, later, Kaltenbrunner.
2. He had the authority to reject any appeal.
3. Ribbentrop and the Ministry of Foreign Affairs never bothered him and followed his orders.
4. The Ministry of Transportation always provided him with the necessary means in spite of every difficulty.
5. His men obeyed him blindly.

Another one of Eichmann's close collaborators, Rudolf Höss, commandant at Auschwitz, has left a frightening portrait of the defendant in his autobiography: "Eichmann was a dynamic man, always active. He couldn't rest; he was completely dedicated to the 'final solution'…" He was the only one who knew the precise number of victims. I was never able to get any help from him to mitigate the massacre. The 'final solution' was his lifework."

The prosecution at this point would like to introduce the depositions from the Nuremberg trial given by three Nazis who are now in Germany: Wilhelm Höttl, Eberhard von Thadden, and Walter Huppenkoethen. Servatius objects because since they are alive they could be called to testify at the tribunal in Jerusalem with the necessary guarantees of immunity. Naturally he knows that this is impossible.

The president wisely decides to take some time and delays the decision to the following day.

Then the witnesses keep on coming, according to the prosecution's plan to present the documents that relate to the same period.

Moritz Fleischmann is a seventy-year-old gentleman who lives in England and testifies in German, as did a few preceding witnesses. In 1938, when the Nazis occupied Vienna, he was one of the leaders of the local Jewish community. As the population was welcoming the Nazis enthusiastically, Jewish institutions were shut down and the main leaders were arrested. "At the end of March we were summoned to the Hotel Metropole. There were six of us, but I am the only survivor of that group. An SS officer took us to see Eichmann. He was wearing the black SS uniform and sitting at a long table while we were left to stand. He asked that we introduce ourselves. When he heard the name of Adolf Boehm he asked him: "Are you the author of the *History of Zionism*?" "Yes." "It's a very interesting book," said Eichmann "I have studied it carefully. Especially one chapter." And he recited a whole page from memory. He then added a few words in Hebrew and said: "Don't be surprised… I speak Hebrew and Yiddish well because I was born in Sarona…""

The president interrupted to ask: "What did he say in Hebrew?"

Fleischmann: "I don't know because I don't understand Hebrew…" Even the judges had to keep from smiling. "Eichmann told us that his orders were to solve the Jewish problem in Austria, that he was to clean Vienna and Austria out of their Jewish population."

Eichmann, the small time officer contemptuous and bullying, rude and vulgar, sure of himself in his black uniform behind the ever present desk, also had the pretense to appear to be a well-read scholar of Zionism…this is not so outlandish if one thinks that this false information, just like his equally false statement of being born in Sarona in Palestine, formed the basis of his entire career. He had only read a single book about Zionism (half of it); he only knew a few words of Hebrew, but that was enough for him to be thought of, as early as 1938, as an indispensable expert on Jewish issues, allowing him to have such a brilliant career.

Fleischmann managed to escape from Austria in August 1939, having tasted some of the delights of Nazi occupation: once he was forced by the SS to wash the staircase with water mixed with acid in the company of a rabbi they had dragged out of the synagogue wearing a *tallit* (prayer shawl) on his shoulder. Typical feats of valor by the youthful SS, who were preparing for other kinds of actions.

Dr. Pranz Mayer is the second witness of the day. With degrees in Science, Philosophy, Sociology, and Economics, he had been active in the Zionist movement in Berlin before the First World War. His first meetings with Eichmann began in 1936–37. Eichmann was polite and addressed him as "Sir," asking that he explain the structure of the various Zionist parties. "I had the feeling I was speaking with an official who wanted to learn something."

When Mayer saw Eichmann again he had completely changed. Mayer was part of the group that was summoned to Vienna in February 1939 to see how the Central Emigration Office worked. "I immediately told my colleagues that I could hardly recognize Eichmann. Instead of a bureaucrat who wrote reports, we were facing a man who behaved roughly like a dictator who had the power of life and death over us. He made us stand far from his desk. Then we visited the Central Office. It made a terrible impression. It seemed like an automatic factory or a store or a bank branch. After going through the building you exit without a penny from the other side with a passport and an order to emigrate within two weeks or else be deported to a concentration camp. We met Eichmann once more in the afternoon. We told him a similar system wouldn't work in Berlin and that the Jews should be allowed to leave Germany with a regular passport, a visa, and some money so as not to be an immediate burden on the new country. Eichmann yelled insults at one of our group because he kept his hands in his pockets and answered that we would discuss that in Berlin." Just a few months before the mass shootings and the gas chambers, Jewish leaders in Berlin were still frantically attempting to have a normal discussion with Eichmann about passports, visas, and money, "as we had always done…" Perhaps in this blindness, in the desire to disbelieve up to the last minute the markers of a fate that was already at hand, the same attitude that will be found later in Warsaw or in Rome, helps explain in part the enormous dimensions of this tragedy.

Thursday, April 27

The long set of documents that Deputy Prosecutor Bar-Or placed on record at this morning's hearing has deeply bored the public and the newsmen. The president must have also felt the same way because as he opened the afternoon hearing he said: "Mr. Bar-Or you have introduced some fifty documents this morning. In normal procedure this should take about one hour. Instead, it took you the entire morning. If things keep on going at this pace the trial will take too long, which is something we wish to avoid. Therefore, in the future only brief citations from the documents you will produce will be allowed. With respect to the witnesses, we must also avoid repeating issues that do not have a direct bearing on the defendant's responsibility."

The chiding was perhaps harsh but well deserved, and this presiding judge pulls no punches when it comes to the prosecution.

The documents include SS orders, lists of SS officers, reports that clarify the attitude of the German foreign ministry regarding Jewish emigration in 1938, and letters from Göring and Heydrich. There is a report from Heydrich, dated November 11, 1938, regarding the "*Kristallnacht*," where one can read the following summary: "Eight hundred fifteen shops destroyed, two hundred seventy-seven synagogues destroyed or burned, twenty thousand Jews arrested, thirty-six Jews killed, and thirty-six more seriously wounded." Then there is a report compiled by Herbert Hagen regarding the trip he took with Eichmann to Palestine and Egypt in September-October 1937. "The economic situation in Palestine is hopeless," he wrote, "since the Jews are endlessly trying to mislead one another and without Aryans are unable to organize their own economy." There are also a few letters from Eichmann in Vienna to Hagen that the Americans found in SD archives. "Tomorrow I shall visit the Jewish community and the Zionists. I do this about once a week. By now they are completely in my hands. I think I will be appointed to head a subsection. I would not want to leave Vienna since I enjoy this work. I feel at home here. But you must understand that at 32, I have no intention of retiring and my superior understands this…" This was what interested Eichmann most on May 8, 1938—his career, first and foremost.

Now the witnesses for the prosecution continue. Today they will recall the second part of Eichmann's brilliant career: Czechoslovakia. David Meretz was the president of the Czech Zionist Federation when on March 15, 1939, the Nazis marched into Prague. "It was just before the world war and the Gestapo was pressuring us to step up emigration. But we didn't have enough certificates for Palestine and the only solution was illegal emigration. In the meantime Eichmann had opened the Central Emigration Office in a house owned by Jews on the outskirts of Prague. There was a group of employees there and whoever wished to emigrate had to pay taxes to the ministry of finance. Then he would provide a list of his possessions and paid a tax equal to 100 percent of their value. Jewels were estimated and placed in a bank. Whoever had a dog had to go to an office and pay the tax on dogs. It was a very long and humiliating procedure. Three or four weeks later the letter would come saying that the passport was ready. But before you could get it you often had to pay another hundred thousand crowns to one of the German officials."

Malka Zimer was an employee of the Central Emigration Office set up by Eichmann with his assistant Günther as manager. "One day in 1940 they told us Eichmann was going to visit. There were no people left with an emigration visa and the Central office was empty. Günther immediately assembled about one hundred Jews, gave them dockets and lined them up to create the illusion that everything was proceeding normally. Eichmann was very pleased with his inspection tour."

Today's last witness, Max Burger, was expelled from Czechoslovakia on October 17, 1939. "They put us in a train and sealed the cars. We had nothing to eat or drink for three days. Finally we reached Nisko, a railroad stop on the Krakow-Lublin line in Poland. A group of SS officers was waiting on the platform and one of them gave a speech that said, more or less, "Seven or eight kilometers from here the Führer has promised a new homeland for the Jews. There are no houses; build them and you shall have a roof. There is no water and the wells are polluted. But you shall dig and have water." Some of us had already met that SS officer in Prague: it was Eichmann. The new homeland was a bare windswept plateau. By evening we finished setting up a barracks for the guards while we remained out in the open. In the winter the temperature went down to forty degrees below zero (centigrade). Each day we had to go and get water from a village many kilometers away. It was assigned by right first for the guards, then the horses, then finally for us. In April 1940 the three hundred who were still in the camp were suddenly sent back to Czechoslovakia. The others had attempted in the meantime to cross the border with Russia that was close by. Eichmann looked younger, he was in uniform, wore no glasses, but I have no trouble recognizing him."

The Nisko experiment was brought to an end as Wisliceny recalled in his testimony. But Max Burger's ordeal was not over and in 1944 he was deported to Auschwitz with his entire family.

Friday, April 28

Today's hearing reached its most dramatic climax toward the end as Mrs. Ada Lichtmann took the stand and said that at age twenty she saw her father killed in front of her. Eichmann, who was very active and busy when the documents were being discussed, is now completely indifferent to the witness, whom he hardly looked at from behind his plastic rimmed glasses.

With an oddly calm voice, her eyes hidden behind dark glasses and speaking Yiddish mixed with some Polish, Ada Lichtmann remembered the executions and massacres of which she was an eyewitness. She then opened the "Poland" chapter after Austria and Czecho-slovakia that we heard during the preceding days. We shall summarize what Public Prosecutor Hausner had to say about Poland during his opening statement.

The Extermination in Poland

…Slavic peoples were considered an inferior race by Nazi doctrine. As for the Jews, their situation was infinitely worse. The only difference of opinion about them between the General Government of Poland and the RSHA had to do with the date of the extermination. While Governor Frank wanted to use the Jews to manufacture weapons and munitions and eliminate them only later, the Gestapo took the initiative of killing them immediately. Frank protested because the Gestapo was taking action within his jurisdiction and he demanded that they at least let him have the skilled workers, but Eichmann and his department went ahead with their destructive mission without paying attention to him.

The Jews began to suffer in Poland as soon as the Nazis arrived. Thousands were killed, the synagogues burned down, and the elders were forced to sign a document saying that they had torched them themselves. Religious Jews were forced to dance around the burning sacred books and often their beards were yanked off with the skin. But all this remained part of the time of the "minor terror."

On December 12, 1939, Heydrich appointed Eichmann to supervise the evacuation of the Jews from the eastern regions. The Jews were to be deported and those regions were to be repopulated with Germans. From then on Eichmann was acting in the east in Himmler's name. In a few months he was able to deport into the General Government half a million Jews. At the same time the first ghettos were set up. Overcrowding quickly caused epidemics and the ghetto itself became a method of extermination. To attempt to leave the ghetto meant being hanged in public. In Warsaw in 1940 in a few days one hundred thousand Jews were forced to move into the Jewish quarter not knowing where they were going to live. The ghetto was then sealed by a wall and thousands more Jews from the provinces were also dumped there. Life there became impossible. The awful sanitary conditions and the lack of food caused the initial deaths. Children were roaming around at night begging for a piece of bread. Hundreds of Jews were buried every day. Round-ups began in the street at random and fathers were deported in front of their children. Taking advantage of the hunger, the Nazis told the Jews to show up voluntarily for deportation in exchange for three kilos of bread and one kilo of jam.

Work camps were another way to eliminate people where the efforts required and the conditions the prisoners were being kept in were such that most of them died in the process. As head of the IV B4 section and special commissioner for the extermination of the Jews, Eichmann was directly responsible as the instigator and organizer of this bloodbath. We shall prove his responsibility in the creation of the ghettos and extermination camps. Even though he was involved in the Heydrich plan, Eichmann also handled small matters; for example, the hanging of seven Jews in the presence of the population of the ghetto of Czechanow.

"In this trial against Adolf Eichmann," said Hausner, "we will not be able to describe the Warsaw ghetto revolt in detail. However, it shall forever remain in Jewish history as an act of supreme courage, the final desperate struggle of a group of heroes who managed to hold their positions for over one month while facing the powerful German army. Even after any organized resistance came to an end they kept on fighting amid the ruins until the last fighters died in September 1943. However, Warsaw was not the only place where the Jews organized their resistance against their oppressors. Even inside the death camps, in the gas chambers of Treblinka, Sobibor, and Auschwitz, revolts took place. Thousands of Jews joined the partisan units and were responsible for innumerable acts of bravery. Israel grieves their death and will transmit their memory to all its children…"

But let us return to the testimony of Ada Lichtmann. "In 1939 I was in Wiseliczka," she began. "I can remember the pretty little village of Wiseliczka, a few kilometers outside Krakow, with its rock salt mine that is among the most famous in Europe. A few hundred meters underground an entire church was built in the salt with chandeliers and statues, also made of salt. Further down at seven hundred meters the walls and the tunnels show the marks of fossils and fish that filled the region one million years ago when it was underwater.

"One day," the witness went on, "a few SS assembled thirty-two Jews in the market place, my father among them. They forced them to take their clothes off and march around the square yelling: "We are filthy Jews, traitors to Germany." Then they were put on a truck that took off immediately. I ran after it for six kilometers but only managed to catch up with it in Tashiz forest. The Jews, in groups of five, were sprawled on the ground, stained in blood. With them were also four Poles who had been taken along the way. They had all been shot. I ran to my father's body and kissed him, but he was already cold. I returned to the village and called some people to help me bury the dead. A few days later I moved to Krakow." The witness kept on telling her story in a monotone. "At Mialicz they herded the Jews into the synagogue and set fire to the building. Those who attempted to flee from the windows were shot on the spot. We were taken by the SS and sent to a factory. To melt the snow and let a child drink we had to bribe the guards with some of our valuables. Children who cried were killed and their parents attempted to cover their mouths. A short time later from my window in Dubinka I saw about twenty religious Jews assembled, wearing their holiday clothes with their prayer shawls on their shoulders and prayer books in their hands. They were ordered to pray and sing a few psalms; then the officers doused them with gasoline and set them on fire."

Before her testimony Jacob Kratki, a doctor, had testified about the Nisko experiment, the same one that another witness, Max Burger, had recalled yesterday. He also remembered the little speech Eichmann gave when they reached Nisko, but he was unable to identify the defendant.

As the hearing began the presiding judge read the court's decision regarding former Nazi witnesses currently abroad. The court was unable to grant them immunity nor could it give them entry visas; therefore, even though their appearance in court would be desirable, the court will accept the questioning of these witnesses in the countries where they are located, by a representative for the prosecution and one for the defense.

Monday, May 1

Five witnesses told the judges about their personal experiences of the Nazi persecutions in Poland. The first incident of this trial took place during the morning session. Inside the courtroom, seated in one of the last rows, a man suddenly jumped to his feet and began screaming: "My entire family... You killed everyone, bloodthirsty dog..." The presiding judge ordered that he be escorted out of the courtroom and the guards did their best to quiet him down. He was let back in about one hour later. In itself the incident is not surprising; it actually made us aware of the fact that until now the trial had taken place with an audience that was so subdued as to give the impression it was absent.

Zvi Pachter, today's first witness, described one of those tragic marches when they were being transferred, in the course of which many were killed on the sides of the road. Pachter's march was certainly among the first: on a Saturday morning in December 1939 the Jewish men of Rubishov were assembled on the square and the march began "A girl followed us, screaming 'Father!' but she was taken away. If anyone grew tired he'd be taken out of the line and we would hear a gunshot. There were no roads and often we would sink into the mud up to our knees. The SS always had us sleeping outside. The guards would be switched every half hour, since they were unable to keep with the pace we had to follow. It was almost a race. We were about two thousand. By the third day the number of dead was already high. Many were so tired they would just give up. Others had their feet mangled but refused to stop for fear of being shot on the spot. Near the border the SS ordered us to run on a bridge where there were Soviet sentries at the other end. But the Russians pushed us back. Only during a second attempt did we manage to get through at Sokol in the Soviet zone. Out of the original two thousand there were about one hundred left."

Yaakov Gurfein remained in Sanok in Galicia until July or August 1942 when the Gestapo ordered that all the Jews should report to them. "Ten thousand of us were transferred to a camp nearby. Five hundred who didn't report in time were killed in a common ditch. We were told not to fear anything since the Führer had ordered a stop to the deportations and they needed us as workers for the war. They added that we were not to escape and that there would be no more killings or deportations. We worked like that for a few months and in January 1943 we were placed in box cars. In our car there were one hundred three persons and we had to take turns to sit down. Everyone had to relieve himself in front of the others and there were men, women, and children inside. Once the train took the track toward Belsen we understood that we were also on our way to that death camp. Some attempted to jump off the train from the windows, but on the roof of each car there was an SS guard with a machine gun and from time to time we would hear a volley. My mother pushed me out so I jumped. I would never see her again. The train stopped and they shot at me but I was able to hide in the snow for two hours. Then the train started up again. I was safe."

Noah Zabludowicz returned to his village on the border with East Prussia from Warsaw at the start of the war. The train stopped at a station near his village and the German station master ordered all the Jews off the train. No one moved. He then ordered all the travelers to line up on the platform. "There was a Jewish woman next to me carrying a child. The station master asked her if she was Jewish but she pretended to not understand. He killed her and her daughter right there; then he had the train leave the station."

An isolated episode, one of many, but that indicates how a few days after the war began every German, even the stationmaster in a small railroad stop, took it upon himself to kill Jews for his personal satisfaction. It becomes clear that without men of this kind, Eichmann could never have fulfilled his plans as completely as he did. Zabludowicz then describes the forced labor, the humiliations and the torture visited upon the Jews of Czechanow in 1940–41. "We had welcomed four other families into our house and they slept in double-decker beds. One night the SS came into the house and had everyone get out of their beds. Then, with their guns pointed, they forced the men and women to have sex with the husbands and wives of the others in front of their children." In May 1942 Zabludowicz was flogged with the cat o' nine tails and thrown in jail for failing to take off his cap in front of two German soldiers. "One day they took me to the Gestapo command to be questioned. They wanted me to tell them the names of those who were listening to Radio London. I told them that I didn't know. They had me on my stomach on the floor and two Germans started to flog me with metal-studded whips. I made a tremendous effort and broke the chair they had placed over me. Then they started to hit me with the armrests until they were broken. At one o'clock they went off to eat. I begged the guard to finish me off. "You dirty dog! It would be a shame to waste a bullet on you," he answered. A little later the officers were back with a black box as big as a telephone. They tied two lines to my hands and began turning the handle. I felt an electric shock go through my body with increasing intensity. My arms would rise up by themselves. I don't know how I was able to make it through. After one hour they took me back to my cell."

We were lined up on November 5, 1942, to be deported to Auschwitz. A woman near me was holding a child a few months old in her arms and the baby began to cry. An SS guard approached her and said: "Please give me your child." The woman was reluctant but the kindly manner convinced her. He took the baby and slammed its head on the pavement, killing it. The mother was unable to cry."

Zabludowicz has completed his testimony but he could go on for hours. Servatius has no questions for the witness. By the usual phrase, *Keine Frage* (no questions), the defense wishes to create the impression that all this testimony may be pitiful personal anecdotes but they have nothing to do with the defendant. However, immediately after this witness, Hausner introduces document n. 1254: a telegram in which Eichmann ordered "special treatment" for four Jews from Czechanow, the same ones that the witness saw being hanged in the main square. Finally, Eichmann appears concerned and no longer seems bored; his face is twitching.

Moshe Bensky, now a magistrate in Tel Aviv, has described the work camp near Krakow where he was being held prisoner in 1943-44.

"Not a day went by in the camp without a death or a killing. We were often brutally whipped and we had to count the blows out loud. If we made a mistake they started all over again. Once a man who had screamed as they were flogging him had to go and thank the camp commander for the punishment and when he turned around they shot him in the back. The commander enjoyed shooting from his window at those working near his beautiful house. In October 1944 all twenty thousand prisoners were assembled on the main plaza. There were also one hundred eighty children. A train appeared in the distance and the mothers began screaming as the children were taken away. The machine guns of the SS were cocked and ready: we heard the clicking. And while the children were being dragged away the camp loud-speakers were broadcasting sweet lullabies."

"But why didn't you attempt to revolt if you were about twenty thousand Jews facing a few hundred SS?" asks the attorney general. It is the question that all the *Sabras*, the young people who were born in Israel, ask, since they can't understand such submissive behavior.

"It is very difficult to answer," says Bensky. "Those who haven't gone through such an experience will have trouble understanding. It was already, in 1943, over three years since the war broke out. We each felt a terror inside that is hard to explain. And then, where could we go dressed in rags with our shaved heads? At that time we did not yet know what had happened to our families who had been deported and we were hoping that by working they would manage to save their own lives. I can't find the right words to express our state of mind. I could have escaped easily enough because I worked in town every day in Krakow. But how could I escape knowing that seventy to eighty people inside the camp, including two of my brothers, would be killed the day after I had fled? In those conditions you did not escape even when it was possible."

In the afternoon following the introduction of a few documents a new witness is called to testify, a young scientist who is living in the United States: Leon Wells. The list of his scientific titles and the positions he held is a bit long and the presiding judge with his benevolent and biting way attempted to cut it short. However, Wells' testimony became one of the more interesting ones of the trial. In

1941, when the Germans occupied Lwow, Wells was sixteen: "After ten days I was arrested along with my father and five thousand other Jews. We were forced to lay on our stomachs on the ground for one whole day without moving a finger. At night we could hear the screams of those who were beaten. By morning about one hundred Jews lay in the courtyard with their brains scattered from the beatings. Then the trucks began to take us away. The following evening there were one hundred fifty of us left. They made us run, beating us relentlessly until finally they went away. I was arrested a second time a few days later and sent to the Janowska camp. One morning eight young men were plunged naked into a big vat of water with the excuse that they were dirty. By the following day the corpses were enclosed in a tomb of ice. The camp commander amused himself with a strange form of target practice: while the internees were dragging very heavy rocks up and down he would shoot at them, aiming at a nose or a finger. By evening the wounded were finished off with a bullet in the back of the neck. At times he enjoyed strangling a prisoner with his own hands.

"I became sick with typhus and pneumonia. I fell and was unable to work. They put me with a sick group and we were ordered to march toward the sand dunes outside the camp. While we were on our way the burial squad caught up with us and our fate became clear. We were told to take our clothes off and get registered. Then we began digging our own pits. Two men would lie down in the pits and be shot dead. The two that followed were told to throw some sand over the dead then to lie down over them and be shot as well. When my turn came they suddenly ordered me back to the camp to bring back the corpse of a man who had been killed there. I then managed to hide and once I was certain that they thought I was dead and that my fellow inmates would not be subjected to any reprisals, I fled the camp."

The precise, almost scientific tone of his testimony made a lasting impression. In his booth Eichmann is the only one who seems to have no emotions: to him those things are not new at all! Wells will continue his account tomorrow morning: the description of his ordeal will take another entire morning.

Tuesday, May 2

At the start of the session Servatius makes an attempt to silence the witness arguing that his testimony is not pertinent, but the objection is overruled and Wells continues this morning with his hallucinating account. He is a tall, thin man who looks younger than his age of thirty-six and who managed to have a brilliant scientific career in the United States where he obtained degrees in mechanical engineering and physics.

"In 1942, when I arrived at Sianov," Wells went on, "I found out that my grandfather and my whole family had been deported to Belsen. I tried to commit suicide but was saved by my uncle; he said I had to live and tell the world what had happened. I was returned to the Janovska concentration camp. Only a few hundred Jews out of eight thousand were selected to go to work and I was among them. We would go out in the morning and return in the evening to the music of an orchestra made up of some sixty Jewish prisoners from the camp. The orchestra was to play even during each execution.

In June 1943 I became part of *Sonderkommando 1005*, a team that had the task of covering up the traces of the Nazi massacres. We were to reopen the pits, burn the corpses, grind down the bones and from the ashes retrieve the gold teeth and wedding rings. After that we were to seed the ground to prevent any kind of discovery. The number of bodies dug up and burned was to match a list of those that had been killed. At times it took hours to locate a corpse because it had been buried separately. We made stacks of about two thousand bodies at a time and would gather 3 to 10 kilos of gold every day. When they brought in new victims the numbers were even greater. Sometimes the bodies they would throw into the fire would move and scream because they were still alive.

"We were supposed to burn everything very thoroughly. The ashes were sifted and the bones ground up. One month later we opened the pit where I was meant to be buried and we searched for the missing body for two days. The list was so precise that not only did it provide the number of corpses but also the exact position in the pit.

"On our way back from work we were told to sing as we marched. A fireman was in the lead wearing a special uniform and a hook in his hand. Later on we were even accompanied by an orchestra. A man called Brell, who was with me in the Death Brigade, had to place his two daughters, sixteen and eighteen years old, whose bodies were still warm, on the stake.

"Those who were part of the Brigade were changed every eight to ten days and had to be killed. But our commander decided to keep us a bit longer to get things done faster."

The presiding judge objects to the length of the testimony but the prosecutor explained that this was one of the few witnesses in the world able to recount the procedure used to cover up the traces which is by itself proof of guilt. Wells therefore continues with the account of his harrowing odyssey.

"One night we decided to escape. To cover up our flight the musicians were to play as loud as they could. They knew they would be killed but they agreed to perform anyway, since none of us cared anymore about who would survive. All we wanted was for one of us to stay alive and tell the world what had happened. Some remained who had decided to be killed: having lost their entire family they no longer wished to live. On the other hand, when we escaped into the forests many of us were killed by Polish partisans. I don't know to which political group they belonged but I do know that they were anti-Semitic. Some people did help us but the overwhelming majority of the Polish and Ukrainian population of Lvov was against us. Out of five hundred thousand Jews only two hundred managed to survive. During the war I kept a diary that was published in Poland after the liberation."

Wells has now finished; the judges are worn out. Among the documents that were introduced after recess there is a deposition by Höss where *Sonderkommando 1005* is specifically referred to as being under the command of Globel, who reported to Eichmann.

Henryk Ryss, a zincographer from Tel Aviv, testifies regarding conditions in the Lodz ghetto. During the massive deportation in 1942 one hundred twenty thousand Jews were shipped to the death camps. To move things faster the SS threw children from one to ten years old out of the windows of the Jewish hospital. "I used to be a photographer inside the ghetto and I took many illegal pictures. In 1944 I hid them in a hole with some friends so that if anyone of us was to be alive he could find them for history." The pictures that we retrieved are put into the record: they show children who had died of hunger, women about to be deported, and Jewish police agents. This man risked his life in order to document for future generations the gigantic tragedy endured by his people.

Servatius now asks to introduce four witnesses for the defense: Doctor Six, who was the head of RSHA Section II; Max Merten, councilor to the military government in Salonika; Hermann Krumey, who took Eichmann's job in Hungary; Eberhard von Thadden, a department head at the Ministry of Foreign Affairs. All four are in Germany and according to the defense they should be testifying that Eichmann couldn't act on his own initiative but only on orders coming from his superiors. Krumey is the only one who is now in prison, but all four could be placed under arrest in Israel. The only solution will be to question them abroad through an itinerant commission.

The next to last witness of this tiring day is the medical doctor Yosef Bvzhminsk, who was saved thanks to a Polish woman who became his wife. He recalls his experience in the Przemysl ghetto, filled with random shootings, children killed in front of their mothers and deportations. It sounds like a different version of the same story. Yet there was also an amazing moment. "In the ghetto I saw a boy being whipped. Usually fifty lashes were enough to kill a young man. But he was able to hold on and after eighty lashes they told him to run. He managed to run and that saved his life." "Do you recognize that boy in this courtroom?" Asked the prosecutor "Yes, he is the police officer sitting next to you!" It was Commissioner Goldman, who took part in section "06" during the preparation of the material for the trial. The audience voiced its surprise and the presiding judge had trouble calling it to order.

Finally, Israel Carmel, a Tel Aviv magistrate, tells of his research regarding the diary, some thirty-eight volumes, of Hans Frank, who had been the governor general of Poland. This time Servatius uses his right to cross examine the witness and asks: "How many times is Eichmann's name cited in the thirty-eight volumes, sir?" "Not once," was Carmel's reply and Servatius sat down, visibly satisfied with his small success.

Wednesday, May 3

Today's hearing was entirely devoted to the revolt of the Warsaw ghetto, an extremely interesting subject even though Judge Landau began by asking the prosecutor to limit himself to the bare minimum.

The facts themselves are well known by now and were published during the last few years in many articles, and books. But as they are told by the protagonists themselves they take on a new meaning—the mark of authenticity. The characters and the historical facts come together and complete the various versions, offering a vivid summary of the most important Jewish revolt against the Nazis, or at least the one that is best remembered.

If the testimony regarding the Warsaw ghetto is somewhat removed from the well-defined limits of legal procedure, they do however belong within the spirit of the trial. It was said many times that this trial was mainly intended for the younger generation so that they may find out and understand. Today's hearings are essential in that respect; Zivia and Yitzhak Zuckerman are fighters, against the Nazis then and against nature today. Their vocabulary is that of the youth born in Israel and who shall understand that in the end there cannot be a simple, clear-cut answer to their most common question that resonates in the courtroom and that they repeat so frequently: why did you go like sheep to the slaughter without even a desperate attempt at resistance?

Each of the witnesses of the last few days gave a personal explanation to that question. Some remembered the sheer terror, the fear of torture, and the desire to die in peace. Others recalled the solidarity with their family and their fellow workers on the teams who would have paid with their lives any attempt to escape. It is clear from their words that the Nazis had gone through a careful psychological preparation, planning for every possibility, even the post-dated cards to be sent to the parents long after those signing them had been gassed.

Zivia Lubetkin was, along with her husband Yitzhak Zuckerman, one of the leaders of the Jewish underground in Warsaw and today lives in the kibbutz Lohamei Haghettaot ("The ghetto fighters").

With its black-and-white cows and blond-haired children, the kibbutz is very much like any commune. However, anyone observing it carefully will immediately see not far from the road connecting Acco to the Lebanese border the recently built Museum of the Resistance.[17] Coming from eighty-nine different ghettoes, the founders of the kibbutz managed to do with very limited funds what state-sponsored and far larger institutes have taken over ten years to accomplish. They created a museum of the resistance and massacre that in a few square meters gives the Israelis an idea of the suffering of the European Jews.

Zivia Lubetkin, who has already published a book of memoirs, is sure of herself and articulate and speaks without any flourishes. She told the story of the Warsaw ghetto from its creation in 1940, when the Germans had promised social and cultural autonomy to the Jews. "To the half million Jews shut inside, the ghetto had turned into a vast prison. The awful overcrowding with fourteen to fifteen people per room and the lack of water were the cause of the initial epidemics. Hunger also took its victims and in the morning you could see the bloated corpses covered with paper because their clothes had been stolen during the night. The Jew in the ghetto was alone and abandoned in front of the Nazis while we were only a small number but organized. Whoever found a potato would share it with his comrades. Someone who for months and months has survived on a slice of bread and a bowl of soup per day thinks only of food. Yet we Zionists managed even to create illegal schools and seminaries in 1941! By the end of that year the first news of the massacres came from two different sources.

"First a Polish man came and told the story how at Vilna the Nazis killed thousands of Jews, including women and children. Then came a Jew who had escaped from the extermination camp at Chelmno. He told us how the Jews were put in a truck and gassed. A rabbi who heard his story said he was crazy. But we believed him. We understood

---

17. Now known as The Ghetto Fighters' House (full name: Itzhak Katzenelson Holocaust and Jewish Resistance Heritage Museum and Study Center).

that what was happening in the east was part of a pre-ordained plan. Cultural activities were interrupted and we devoted ourselves entirely to preparing the resistance. The others who were the majority just could not believe that an entire nation could be exterminated.

"Then the deportation began. We found out that the destination was the nearby camp of Treblinka. Using hunger as bait the Nazis invited the Jews to volunteer to be deported. By the end of 1942, out of the initial half million, only sixty thousand Jews were left inside the ghetto. In the meantime the Jewish fighter organization was created, led by Mordechai Anilewicz. We prepared military posts everywhere." Zivia lived at 33 Nalewsky Street, one of the typical streets of Warsaw's Jewish quarter when I saw it, full of life with its thousand shops and outside stands in 1938. Mordechai Anilewicz was at 29 Mila Street.

"On April 18 we were told that the Germans were preparing an action. We gave the final orders and proclaimed the alert. By morning I saw thousands of Germans attack the ghetto using heavy machine-guns as if they were at the Russian front. We were about twenty men and women armed with one pistol, two rifles, and some homemade bombs you had to light up with a match in order to detonate. We knew that we were close to the end but we were happy because we intended to make them pay a high price for our lives. But we were even more overjoyed when a miracle occurred: the Nazi "heroes" retreated in the face of our attacks without even taking their wounded. We could finally see fear in their eyes.

"They came back of course, with the support of their tanks. During the first few days the Germans had hundreds of dead. The fighting went on and our bunkers fell one after another. The one at 18 Mila Street fell on May 8, 1943 and Mordechai Anilewicz was killed. The only way out was through the sewers into the Aryan part of town."

Her husband, Yitzhak Zuckerman, testified after her; he is a handsome, tall man in his forties who drags his leg a bit since it was hit by a German bullet. He has blond hair and thick mustache—basically an Aryan look that saved his life. At the kibbutz they still refer to him deferentially as "the commander"; he is one of the ten survivors of the Warsaw ghetto, where he was second in command.

Zuckerman tells how he escaped from a concentration camp at the beginning of the occupation and became one of the leaders of the Jewish underground. His task was to keep communications open among the various communities within the "General Government" of Poland.

A sudden power failure forces the court to interrupt the hearing, which given its importance is being broadcast throughout the country today. As the audience slowly comes out of the dark courtroom, the only remaining light is the neon inside Eichmann's booth, obviously supported by an emergency power system.

The electricity then returns and Zuckerman resumes his testimony. "The Jewish [fighting] organization that included all the Zionist movements and the Bund was founded in 1942. But we were totally isolated from the rest of the world. El Alamein and Stalingrad did not exist for us.

"In December 1942 I traveled to Krakow. On Christmas Eve we planned an armed attack on a café that catered to the Germans. The attack was a success but I was wounded in the leg. Once I recovered I returned to the Warsaw ghetto and attempted to contact Polish partisans who at the time were not yet well-organized. A small revolt in January 1943 taught us an important lesson that we applied later during the April uprising: we should not allow ourselves to give battle in the streets, but instead we should adopt a partisan tactic and fight house to house. Some even proposed that we set fire to the whole ghetto to die in the flames. I disagreed because I didn't intend to hand over our lives to the Nazis so cheaply.

When the uprising took place in April 1943 I had been in the Aryan sector for six days to find weapons for my fellow fighters. I managed to secure twenty-two rifles from the "Armia Ludowa" (The Polish People's Army) and slip them in under the noses of the guards with the help of the undertakers. On April 23 I received a letter written in Hebrew from Mordechai Anilewicz. He wrote: "Dear Izhak: Something has happened beyond our wildest dreams. The Germans fled the ghetto twice! Now we hide during the day and have night raids to capture weapons. My life's dream is becoming reality: I have seen Jewish self-defense in all its splendor."

Zuckerman secured a map of the sewers that turned out to be invaluable to establish communications first and later to rescue the survivors in the ghetto. "It would be a mistake to think that the Warsaw ghetto was the only one to rise up. In many places Jewish fighters attempted to fight even with their bare hands. Resistance was set up in Bialystock and even at Treblinka. The results were different because they didn't wish to abandon the older men and women to their fate by escaping into the forests. We wanted to save our honor, if not our lives."

Zuckerman has finished; his is a testimony Israelis are proud of.

More witnesses testify to life inside the Warsaw ghetto. Dr. Emanuel Ringelblum had begun to collect historical documents about life there, written by various authors as reports meant for a newspaper that didn't exist. An extremely valuable archive was therefore created. In 1946 two workers discovered two milk containers filled with papers under the rubble of a house that was part of the archive hidden long before.

The wife of Dolek Lieberskind, head of Jewish resistance in Krakow, and a runner from his staff, recalled the attack on the café mentioned by Yitzhak Zuckerman, along with other partisan operations. Servatius chooses to not cross-examine the witnesses and becomes concerned when the prosecution introduces a few documents connecting Eichmann to the actions discussed by today's witnesses.

Avraham Berman, a Tel Aviv psychologist, described the massacre of Jewish children in the Warsaw ghetto. He recalled the well-known educator Janosz Korczak, who wanted to accompany the children from his orphanage on their final journey and refused to save his own life. Then he described what he saw at the death camp at Treblinka.

"I arrived there in January 1945, shortly after the liberation. You could see bones and skulls scattered everywhere by the hundreds of thousands, over several kilometers, including mountains of shoes, with the smaller children's shoes among them. Here, they are for you to see." Two small shoes. Some people in the audience are unable to hold back their tears.

The Extermination in the Soviet Union and the Baltic States

Thursday, May 4

Today's hearing will be dedicated to persecutions in the Soviet Union. Here is a summary of Public Prosecutor Hausner's opening statement at the beginning of the trial.

"All Jews were to be killed but the methods would change depending upon the location where they were living. In the Soviet Union the RSHA's orders to the action squads (*Einsatzgruppen*) were to kill all the Jews, along with Communist party officials. We shall introduce reports that in terse bureaucratic language discuss the mass murders. The testimony of Otto Ohlendorf, who was in charge of *Einsatzgruppe D* is as follows: "Men, women, and children were taken near an anti-tank ditch. Then they were killed. I ordered my men to always shoot at the same time to avoid personal responsibility. Early in 1942 the head of the security police, the SD, sent us some buses that could kill, using gas, within ten to fifteen minutes." It is almost impossible to believe that for months on end thousands of Nazis murdered in cold blood with their own hands some seven hundred fifty thousand Jews and that such human beasts had even walked on the face of the earth.

The victims arrived in long columns and were killed with their clothes on. Later the system changed. Paul Flobel was part of Eichmann's section and described an execution: "As they got off the truck, men, women, and children of all ages had to undress and their clothes were piled up according to their category. No one begged for pity. Families remained together; a father held the hand of his ten-year son and was speaking to him in a low reassuring voice as he pointed to the sky. They were marched to the pit in groups of twenty by an SS handling a whip. Another SS was waiting for them, his legs dangling over the side of the pit with a machine gun between his knees and a cigarette eternally stuck in his mouth. The completely naked people went into the pit and would lie down over those already there. At times one of those bodies would still be moving.

"Eichmann personally took care of the ghettos of Riga and Minsk where thousands of German Jews were deported. They had been told that they were to colonize the area and would be doing agricultural work. They were all exterminated. But even as they came up to the side of the pit the Jews remained deeply immersed in centuries-old traditions. In a book entitled *Answers from the Deep* the Kovno rabbis were recording the opinions they offered day after day on issues such as: What should a Jew do if he were ordered to tear up the Scrolls of the Laws? Is it allowed to wear clothing belonging to the dead? Is abortion allowed if the pregnancy will lead to the mother's execution?

"Eichmann also handled individual cases such as that of Mrs. Cozzi, who was deported to Riga…"

But let's return to today's hearing. The morning session is mostly taken up by Abba Kovner, who was one of the leaders of the partisan struggle in Lithuania and who is currently in a kibbutz. A poet and a noted writer, he is also known in Israel for his activities during the Arab-Israeli War of Liberation of 1948, when he was the political commissar of the "Ghivati." At Negba, which was the last outpost in the south on the road to Tel Aviv, the brigade and the kibbutz people were to hold for several weeks, in defiance of any kind of military logic, against an enemy many times stronger with tanks and regular army weapons. Through his moving daily statements and slogans from the partisan war, like "Death to the enemy invaders!" Kovner played an important part in that struggle.

As he took the witness stand this morning with his unruly thick head of hair, his mesmerizing look and the simple but deliberate words he uses, a sense of excitement ran through the audience all the way to the back row. Many others were following on television from the next room. President Ben Zwi later expressed the emotion he felt as he listened to Kovner's testimony.

Kovner returned to the ruins of the Vilna ghetto in July 1944, leading a Jewish partisan unit fighting with Red Army assault units. He recalls: "In a desert of empty streets a woman holding a three year old child suddenly appeared. As soon as she saw us the woman began crying hysterically. Her daughter, who had seemed to be unable to speak, asked: 'Mother, can we already cry?'"

The witness then describes life in the Vilna ghetto, the first mass executions in Ponar forest in September 1941, and the beginnings of the underground Jewish organization. "There is a scene that years of underground partisan struggle have not erased from my memory. In August 1941 the ghetto was surrounded and the Germans undertook a huge raid. A woman who was holding something in her arms was dragged off by the hair by the SS. She was thrown into the street and the child fell from her arms. One of the two SS men took the child by the leg. The woman crawled at his feet begging for pity. But the German smashed its head several times against the wall. To me this was a revelation of horrors I knew nothing about until then.

"The forests could be a good place to hide. However, they were two hundred kilometers away and to reach them you had to go over not just the ghetto wall but the even thicker wall of hatred of a hostile population and the collaborators. For us young people it wouldn't have been difficult to grab the few weapons we had and escape into the countryside. But we didn't want to save ourselves and abandon our mothers, sisters, and brothers to their fate. We would only do so as a last resort.

"In October 1941 I heard a woman tell the story of the Ponar massacre. There is an episode I would like to relate. In the line of the victims waiting to be killed there was also a young woman with beautiful eyes and long hair named Serna Morgenstern. The SS officer noticed her and ordered her to take a step forward, but she refused to move. Then he said: 'How can this be? You don't wish to live? It's a shame to bury such beauty. Go, don't look back, walk along the road.' The other women were looking at her with envy. Serna hesitated then began walking a few steps, but the officer shot her in the back."

On January 1, 1942, Kovner wrote his first flyer calling for revolt. It ended with the following words: "All the streets of the ghetto lead to Ponar and Ponar means death. Hitler is planning to kill all the Jews in Europe and fate decided that those in Lithuania should be the first victims. We are weak and defenseless but the only response to the massacres is revolt. Better to die as free fighters than to live at the mercy of the oppressor. Let us defend ourselves until our last breath!"

"But organizing resistance was no simple matter. It was not just about shouldering weapons and beginning to shoot. In this courtroom a question is being asked: why did you not rebel? Even though I happen to be one of those who did fight back I reject the criticism that is implied in that question. To set up an organization requires a national authority or a spontaneous internal movement which was impossible given the conditions of paralyzing terror we were in. Only people with the strongest will can accomplish this but those who are desperate no longer have the will. I have seen desperate people commit suicide but I have never seen them become effective fighters. Those who, like ourselves, began what is called a hopeless struggle were people of great faith: there was the feeling that sacrifice did make sense. When we sent out messengers who were risking their lives to go to other ghettos with news of the massacres, the self-righteous in those towns reacted, saying: 'That will never happen here!'

"At the end of 1941 we came in contact with a young German officer of Austrian ancestry who helped us in various ways. One evening while we were waiting for a messenger to return I asked him who the organizers of the extermination were and I quoted a few names that I knew. At one point he answered that all those I had named had nothing to do with the extermination of the Jews. 'There is a dog named Eichmann,' he told me. 'He's the one organizing all this.' It was the first time I heard the name Eichmann."

There was hushed talk in the courtroom. Eichmann keeps on staring straight ahead with his now signature blank look when the "nonpertinent" texts are introduced as evidence. However, he must have felt the blow.

Kovner remembered a significant episode of the partisan struggle. "A woman was living in the Aryan part of town with false documents. She was safe. We asked her to come back and bring explosives into the ghetto. A few days later, with her load of dynamite, she traveled thirty kilometers on foot and blew up a train full of German munitions: the first train to be hit in Lithuania. The Lithuanians, the Russians, the Poles, who had even more opportunities, did not do it. It took a Jewish woman who returned to the ghetto with bloody feet. That woman today is my wife."

Kovner ends with the Wittemberg story. This was the first commander in charge of the underground Jewish organization in Vilna. "The SS arrested our leader Wittemberg in the ghetto after someone ratted on him. We managed to free him. They gave us an ultimatum: if we refused to give him up within six hours, the entire ghetto would be destroyed. Delegations of Jews were appearing at our headquarters saying: 'You can't sacrifice the whole ghetto for one man.' But we would not give in. And that was how we were with our brothers. For one more hour of life the victims were ready to tear each other apart. 'Give the order and we will fight them,' I said. But Wittemberg didn't want to. He gave me his gun and his command. Then he surrendered to the Gestapo. He was tortured for a long time and killed." Kovner ends by saying: "I have only told the truth, but not the whole truth!"

Mrs. Frida Mazia had testified before Kovner She had worked in the Jewish hospital at Sosnovitz during the occupation and described the persecution in that city. "In 1940 there was a rumor going around to beware of a German officer who was born in the colony in Palestine, who could speak Yiddish and Hebrew and knew Jewish customs. I can't remember his name because at that time I was not paying attention…" It was not hard to recognize Eichmann under that description, since years before in Vienna he had boasted knowledge of Yiddish and Hebrew, saying that he was born in Sarona.

Meir Dvrjetzky is a doctor from Tel Aviv who teaches the history of the Holocaust at Bar Illan University. The Germans occupied Vilna in June 1941 and set up the ghetto two months later. Within a few months forty thousand Jews were killed in the nearby Ponar forest. "I was practicing medicine in Vilna at the time. On September 3, 1941, I saw an unkempt woman in the street who looked as though she were crazy. It was Sonia. She came to see me and said that three days before she had been taken to Ponar forest along with ten thousand other Jews. 'It's not a work camp but a place where they kill Jews!' she said. She was with her son. A few Jews next to her were confessing their sins before dying. Then she heard shots and saw blood everywhere. She remained with the bodies of those killed until sunset when she was able to climb out from under the mountain of bodies and escape. A Polish peasant woman covered her wounds and told her: 'Run away with these flowers in your hand: that way they'll think you're a peasant.' When I saw that her wound had ants crawling in it I understood the terrible truth of the massacre. I told my neighbors but they replied that I was causing panic. 'How can it be possible that they should take the Jews like that to shoot them?' That's what they said."

Up until the end the Jews could not and would not believe even when confronted with the evidence. The witness then describes the kaleidoscope of documents and certificates distributed by the Germans to create confusion: pink, blue, yellow. "Then they issued the "Life Card" to those necessary for the war effort. It was a grey certificate valid for a man, a woman, and two children. Additional children had to die and the head of the family had to choose. I was given this certificate as well but I also had a mother. Who should I pick: my mother or my wife? I went to my mother and asked her for advice: 'Mother, you know the situation. I can take either you or my wife. Tell me what I should do.' And my mother replied, 'It's written in the Holy Bible: "The man shall leave his father and mother to go and live with his wife." I shall give my life for your wife. Give her the certificate.' She gave me her final blessing and we parted forever.

"Since I had no children I added my sister to my certificate and an unknown child who was going around asking 'who wants to be my father?'"

The doctor went on describing his attempts to keep a minimum of culture inside the ghetto by organizing schools, theater groups, newspapers, and so on. Illnesses and malnutrition, especially endemic typhus, claimed many victims. "Toward the end of the war they would transfer us from one camp to another, from Estonia to Germany. In March 1945 we were wandering around the forests in Germany when we were liberated by the French. We immediately went to see the commander, but I weighed only thirty-nine kilos and they sent me to the hospital."

Abraham Karasik testified about the ghetto at Bialystock, the resistance it was able to put up, and its destruction. He was then sent into the "death brigades," already described by Wells, that had the task of erasing all traces of the massacres. His *Sonderkommando* was able to dig up twenty thousand corpses and burn them on giant stakes.

Aharon Peretz is a gynecologist and he tells the story of the Kovno ghetto. The Nazis had forbidden pregnancies under penalty of death and he had to perform many abortions to save the mothers. Then the raids on children began. "I saw a mother running after a truck where her three children had been placed. An SS guard told her she could save only one. All three begged her with their arms to take them. But not knowing which one to take she went back alone."

Friday, May 5

At the start of today's hearing the prosecution introduces new documents that tend to connect Eichmann to the events that had previously been told by other witnesses. Among them is a strange bill of lading written with the well-known German efficiency regarding a shipment of one thousand and seven German Jews to the ghetto at Riga. The recipient of the document was Adolf Eichmann. Another paper shows how the Nazis attempted to instigate the Latvians to go on anti-Semitic pogroms. When it became clear that the latter were not motivated enough, the Germans moved on with the massacres. Eichmann admitted during the pre-trial proceedings to having taken part in a meeting with Heydrich in May 1942. The minutes of that meeting were introduced today and show that on that occasion Heydrich issued orders to the *Einsatzgruppen* commanders to destroy the Eastern European Jews. At Nuremberg Gustav Noske, head of *Einsatzgruppen 12*, stated that reports coming from those units were to be sent directly to Eichmann.

Eliezer Karstaat, a Tel Aviv manufacturer, is called to the witness stand. He was in Riga in July 1941, right after the occupation when the shooting of Jews began and continued unabated until the setting up of the ghetto. Two women brought the incredible news to the ghetto concerning the killings: "They were arrested and taken to the outskirts of the town. A large pit was ready. The Jews had to undress and were then shot dead by the SS, using machine guns. Whether they were dead or not they were pushed into the pit where those still alive would suffocate to death. Both women had been spared on one of the top layers of the pit, and at nightfall they got dressed and escaped." In Riga trains of German Jews being deported started coming in and were shot in the outskirts of town. The witness went on: "We tried to set up resistance inside the ghetto but in 1943 the Gestapo found a rifle and a list of three hundred members of the movement. They were immediately killed. In June 1944 a few Hungarian women coming from Auschwitz arrived and we were told about the crematoriums for the first time. By the end of the war, out of one hundred thousand Latvian Jews, there were only eight hundred left."

The witness has finished testifying. Servatius ends his usual *Keine Frage* and asked what had happened during the First World War when the German army occupied Kurland. But the witness was unable to answer since he was just one year old at the time!

A Tel Aviv employee Avraham Aviel testifies now about the activities of the *Einsatzgruppen*. He was born in a Polish village made up exclusively of Jewish peasants. After the occupation all the inhabitants were taken to the Radom ghetto. In May 1942 the Germans assembled about one hundred Jews—the witness' father was among them—and gave them pails. "Once the group reached the outskirts of town my father yelled out: run away now! Some were successful, my father among them. Shortly after that, the ghetto was surrounded by well-armed German troops on motorcycles. My mother, my two brothers, and I were placed in a column with about one thousand other Jews. My mother was reciting the prayer *Shemá Israel* and told us to die as Jews. Near the cemetery they told us to kneel looking down, forbidding us to move even slightly. I looked anyway and noticed a ditch some twenty-five to thirty meters long where the Jews were taken, told to undress, and shot with machine guns. I decided to escape. Not far from us was a group of workers with their pails who had preceded us; one of my brothers was among them. I managed to jump over and I was the only of the column to save my life. One of the workers saw his family on the other side and tried to save them, waving the travel permit he had been given as a carpenter. He was killed on the spot as his lips kept whispering: 'I have the travel permit…'

"My brother and I escaped into the forests and found a partisan unit. In one of our first operations we were able to kill many Germans and Lithuanian policemen. My brother was killed in a nighttime ambush when some twenty Germans suddenly opened fire on us, probably because we were betrayed. I escaped and joined another Jewish partisan unit. Then I went to Hungary, Austria, and Italy in an attempt to get to Palestine. But the British caught me and sent me to a camp in Cyprus. Finally I reached Israel."

The witness scheduled to follow has suffered a heart attack. Servatius requests that defense witnesses be questioned in Germany: three former Nazis, Richard Baer, the last Auschwitz commandant; Walter Huppenkoethen of the Gestapo; and Wilhelm Höttl of the RSHA. The day's hearing ended on the testimony of Haim Beherndt, who told how the Berlin Jews were taken to Minsk and then killed there.

Monday, May 8

Today Rivka Yosselevska testified. She is a middle-aged woman who had been unable to testify last Friday because of a heart attack. In her Russian-accented Yiddish she was able to tell her awful story to the court. She was born in a village near Pinsk where there were some five hundred Jewish families. The Nazis occupied the village in 1941, when the first actions against the Jews began. Then a ghetto was set up and often the men would risk their lives to go and pray in a cellar at dawn. By 1942 the few ghetto survivors were assembled in the main square and herded into a big truck. Those who were unable to fit inside were told to run after it.

"With my child in my arms," Yosselevska relates, "I ran after the truck as hard as I could. Whoever was left behind was killed on the spot. When we reached the destination I saw the people in the truck who had already arrived undressed at the edge of a huge pit. Four SS men, armed to the teeth, began killing the Jews one by one. My daughter asked "Mother did you have me wear my Saturday best in order to die?" The children's suffering was unbearable and I was only hoping that it would all end soon. My father, my mother, and my sisters were told to undress and were killed in front of me. Then it was my turn. An SS man grabbed my daughter from me: I heard a scream and a shot. Then I was shot as well. I fell among the bodies in the pit. At first I thought I was dead and that the heaviness in my head had to be what someone feels in death. But I was suffocating because of the bodies that kept on falling over me so I tried to move and I understood that I was still alive. All I wanted was another bullet that would put an end to my suffering to avoid being buried under the bodies. Finally, I managed to reach the edge of the pit. The Germans had left. I was naked, covered with other people's blood and excrements. I looked for my daughter Merkele's body among the corpses but I was unable to recognize her. Four of us were still alive and we envied those who were already dead. Blood shot up from the pit like spring water and every time I see a fountain today I can't help recalling that scene. I stayed lying down on top of the corpses for three days and nights. Then some shepherds came by and threw stones at me: they couldn't tell whether I was dead or crazy. Finally, a peasant helped me reach the Jews in the forest and I remained with them until the liberation."

Among the documents that were introduced today there were a few German reports regarding actions taking place in the east. One of them was addressed to the usual IV B4, Eichmann's section, and as of November 1941 it boasts of successful Nazi propaganda: "Thanks to our organizational skill the Jews believed until the last moment when they were executed that they were to be transferred to another location."

Then there is a series of documents regarding the case of Mrs. Jenni Cozzi, a Jewish woman from Riga who had married an Italian officer and through marriage had become an Italian citizen. She managed to contact Giurati, the Italian consul in Danzig, and he immediately took an interest in her case and tried to have her freed, but failed. Then a long discussion began between the Italian embassy in Berlin on one side and Eichmann's office on the other through the German Foreign Office. Eichmann's deputy, Rolf Günther, refused to free Mrs. Cozzi "because she could use the conditions inside the ghetto in Riga for an atrocity propaganda campaign. I request that the Italian embassy stop supporting that Jewish woman." Italian authorities continued their pressure and the Fascist Party even tried to approach the Nazi Party. But Eichmann would have the last word. In his letter dated September 25, 1943, he wrote: "Following the new situation in Italy [the armistice] I don't feel that it is necessary to take any further action in this case. I have given orders for the Jewish woman Cozzi to be interned in the camp at Riga. She can now follow the fate of all the Jews."

This is the first part of the chapter regarding Italy that will show the abyss separating the attitude of the Italian authorities from the Nazis.

Deputy Prosecutor Gabriel Bach then began presenting the case of the persecutions in western Europe with a long set of documents that prove Eichmann's responsibility in the depredations and deportations in those areas. We therefore offer a summary of the initial indictment given by the public prosecutor on that subject.

The Extermination in Western, Central, and Southern Europe

In May 1940, immediately following the German occupation of Holland, a special Jewish section was set up at the local Security Office, also using the IV B4 initials, under Wilhelm Zoepf. Anti-Semitic laws were immediately enforced and the Jews were even forbidden to ride a bicycle. Eichmann's solution for children of mixed marriages was simple: they were to be sterilized. But Holland was to be the first country where the Nazis would encounter popular resistance to their criminal acts against the Jews. In February 1941, after the first raids on the Jews, a general strike in Amsterdam was drowned in blood.

Eichmann's office decided that Sephardic Jews (of Spanish or Portuguese origin) were as Jewish as the rest and had to be exterminated as well. While deportations were being set in motion, the confiscation of property was also taking place, including household objects and Jewish-owned works of art. The thieves made sure that the German people in all parts of the country would benefit from this organized looting.

When he found out that some twenty Jews had managed to secure foreign passports allowing them to emigrate, Eichmann issued orders in 1943 to limit as much as possible any contacts between the Jews inside the camps and the outside world.

As for the property belonging to foreign Jews, the territorial principle was established based on the fact that all the belongings of Jews who had been deported would remain the property of their last country of residence. Confiscation and killing were just two sides of the same operation and were to always remain closely connected.

Transports to the east were Eichmann's responsibility and he wrote to the German Foreign Office that he had "assigned for labor at Auschwitz" forty thousand French, forty thousand Dutch, and ten thousand Belgian Jews. It was actually a lie because he added at the same time ten percent more Jews who were not able to work to be exterminated on arrival. About one hundred twenty thousand Jews were deported from Holland and only five thousand returned.

In Norway, Eichmann did everything he could to block the efforts of the Swedish government and wrote to the Foreign Office: "The Swedish government is attempting an obvious trick in naturalizing those Jews…but we must not accept that." Out of one thousand seven hundred fifty Jews, about eight hundred were deported.

In Denmark, King Christian made a personal plea in favor of the Jews. But things changed as of September 1943 and Eichmann sent his deputy, Günther, to prepare a raid. In early October the SS entered Jewish homes but most of them were empty. The Danish people, having been informed of what was planned, had prepared the so-called "little Dunkirk." Students and other volunteers escorted the Jews to the coast where they were taken to Sweden on fishing boats. Most Danish Jews were saved much to the annoyance of Adolf Eichmann, who traveled to Copenhagen himself to find out the reasons for that fiasco.

Eichmann planned the extermination in Belgium as well and he sent Anton Burger to carry it out.

In France a IV B4 office was also set up reporting to Eichmann under Theodore Dannecker then under Heinz Roethke and Alois Brünner, respectively. The deportees were first deported to concentration camps in France, then to the east. The Vichy authorities, headed by Pierre Laval, practically gave the Jews up to their fate. On August 14, 1942, Roethke could already send a report to Eichmann on the deportation of children to the camp at Drancy, about which we will hear further testimony.

Southern France was under Italian occupation. Mussolini was ready to collaborate with the Nazis in the extermination program but some of the Italian civil servants were not enthusiastic and slowed down the operations. With respect to the solution of the Jewish problem in Italy, the Germans decided that Himmler himself would discuss the issue with the Duce. Eichmann bitterly complained about Italian "sabotage" in the occupied countries, in particular in the letter dated February 25, 1943, that was signed by Heinrich Müller but written by the defendant. Ribbentrop also put on strong pressure on the Italian authorities that used delaying tactics, thereby saving thousands of Jews from certain death. Friedrich Robert Boshammer, along with Dannecker, both under Eichmann's orders, were operating in occupied Italy after September 8, 1943. On October 16, 1943, the deportation of the Jews of Rome took place, followed by a wave of arrests in the northern part of the country. Thanks to the help of the Italians who hid many Jews at the risk of their own lives, the hunt did not bear fruit. The Italian clergy also helped and hid many Jews in the monasteries. Even the embassy of the Republic of Salò in Berlin took an interest in the case of Bernard Taubert, a Jew and an Italian citizen residing in Lvov. Eichmann's deputy, Günther, answered: "In the fifth year of the war German authorities have other far more important tasks than to investigate the fate of a deported Jew. It is disgraceful that the embassy of the Fascist Republic should persist in its old habits of asking clarification regarding the Jews."

The anti-Jewish activities of the defendant were felt throughout Yugoslavia. But in Slovenia he also evacuated the non-Jewish population and fourteen thousand Slovenes were deported to Croatia and Serbia.

In Slovakia the defendant's representative found like-minded allies in Prime Minister Bala Tuka and Minister of the Interior Sano Mach. The Church brought pressure to bear in favor of the Jews and some twenty thousand dollars was given to Wisliceny to interrupt the deportations. But in 1944 twelve thousand other Jews were deported and many others were killed on the spot.

Twenty-eight thousand Jews were deported and killed in Romania following Eichmann's orders in 1941. Plans were drawn to deport the balance of Romanian Jews but Eichmann's efforts to go behind the back of the German Foreign Office were criticized by the ambassador to Bucharest, Manfred von Killinger: "I am not surprised by the fact that Mr. Eichmann failed to remain in contact with the embassy since his methods of operation are too familiar to me." But the Romanian authorities had changed their minds by then, and in 1943 the Jews were saved by the Red Army.

In Bulgaria Dannecker signed a "contract" with the Jewish Affairs commissioner in February 1943 to roundup twenty thousand Jews. The transportation was provided by the Germans and to be paid by the Bulgarians. But following the first eleven thousand victims from Thrace and Macedonia the Bulgarian authorities opposed continuing the deportations.

Eichmann sent the notorious Wisliceny to Greece and in March 1943 deportations began out of Salonika. But there was no cooperation to be had in the Italian zone of occupation. Wisliceny went to Athens and managed to have the family of the legal advisor of the Italian embassy, Saul, arrested. The Italians threatened to arrest Wisliceny, and Eichmann reacted by stating that he would go to Himmler because they wanted to arrest a German police official acting under orders. The matter was hushed up but Eichmann kept on complaining: "We demand that the Italians apply the same measures that exist in our occupation zone, meaning the deportation of all the Jews to the east."

Tuesday, May 9

We have been coming to this trial for almost one month, listening day after day to the horrendous accounts that are all too often terrifying. Yet we never were as emotionally challenged as this morning when we heard about the poor children at Drancy. Georges Wellers, a doctor now in charge of the human physiology laboratory at the Sorbonne, told the story today. He was arrested by the Gestapo on December 12, 1941, and that same evening he was to encounter Theodore Dannecker Eichmann's representative in France. In June 1942 he was sent to Drancy concentration camp where two months later children began arriving, one thousand at a time—up to four thousand Jewish children whose parents had already been deported. "They were made to get off the trucks in a hurry; the older ones were helping the little ones. There were even two-to-three year olds who didn't know their own name and were impossible to identify. We attempted to find out or give them a name and put a little tags around their necks. But then we found out that the kids were exchanging them when they played. They were dirty, their clothes were tattered, this one was missing a shoe, that one had no buttons. They were covered with sores and had diarrhea but we didn't even have soap to wash them. They had no spoons and were given soup in empty tin cans but they were too hot and they could not hold them in their hands. Some kids couldn't even speak to say: "I didn't get my soup," and so they went without any. At times a whole room full of kids would wake up at night crying, calling for their mothers. But the most awful thing was to see them being deported. The gendarmes would wake them up at five in the morning, when it was still dark outside, and would forcefully drag the children who were crying, fighting, trying to resist, hugging one another. It was an awful thing to see. None of them ever came back from Auschwitz.

Later on the witness was also deported to Auschwitz where René Blum, the brother of the famous French statesman, died. Dr. Wellers told his odyssey in a book, *From Drancy to Auschwitz*.

The documents presented today illustrate the way Italian occupation authorities in France "sabotaged" the anti-Jewish measures taken by Eichmann and his colleagues.

In a series of reports to Eichmann, Roethke, the Jewish Affairs expert at the Security Police Headquarters in Paris and Dannecker's successor, described the attitude of Italian military authorities. "If we truly want to solve the Jewish problem we must change the attitude of the Italians," writes Roethke, who then goes on to say that the Italians are sabotaging the deportations and refuse to issue special identification cards to the Jews. By mid-February 1943 the French police had arrested two to three hundred Jews near Lyon but the Italian general based in Grenoble asked that they be immediately released. When his request was refused, Italian troops surrounded the barracks with their weapons at the ready.

In another report Roethke complained about the problem in securing the Jews that Eichmann was demanding and he added: "The

French always refer to the example of the Italians. They tell us 'You know how the Italians are behaving: how can we act any differently?'"

On the basis of these reports Eichmann contacted the German Foreign Office to pressure the Italians to change their attitude. In a letter to von Thadden, the Jewish Affairs officer at the Foreign Office, Eichmann requested a meeting with Lo Spinoso, the Italian police inspector who had been sent to the occupied area to review the matter. The embassy in Rome replied that Italian authorities "didn't think such consultations were desirable for the time being."

Roethke kept on complaining about the Italians to Eichmann. He wrote "The Italian position is incomprehensible. The Italian army and police are protecting the Jews with every means at their disposal. The Italian sphere of influence, particularly on the Riviera, has become the Promised Land for the Jews." In another report Roethke writes that a Jew known as Donati has a lot of influence with the Italians and has done much to save the Jews. German agents have attempted to enter the Italian zone in order to kidnap Donati but did not succeed.

Wednesday, May 10

After one month of Nazi horrors illustrated by documents and the witnesses who took the stand this afternoon, we finally heard something different. For once the huge and perfect death machine failed to work and the trap laid by Eichmann for the Danish Jews didn't bear fruit. As we listened to the fair-haired David Melchior, the son of the Chief Rabbi of Copenhagen, we had the impression of going back to the tales of Hans Christian Andersen. The usual characters of fairy tales were all present: the good king, Christian in this case, who managed to save seven thousand Jews in his country by transferring them to nearby Sweden. There is even the good German George Duckwitz, who warned the Jews that they were about to be deported and would later become the first ambassador of the Federal Republic of Germany to Denmark.

But unfortunately Eichmann's failure was only an exception. In Holland out of one hundred forty thousand Jews living in that country when the German occupation began precisely twenty-one years ago, one hundred ten thousand were deported and only six thousand saved themselves. Joseph Melkmann told us that story this morning. He used to teach Latin and Greek in Amsterdam and is now a senior official in the Ministry of Education of Israel. Following the economic restrictions, the exclusion from entering public buildings and traveling on city buses, came the order in 1942 to wear the yellow star. Out of a sense of solidarity many Dutch gentiles also wore it. The deportations began a few days later. No one could believe that all the Jews were to be deported, nor did anyone even begin to imagine what that actually meant.

"It was only in 1944," Melkmann said, "that I met some women who had been at Auschwitz who told me about the gas chambers. I was first sent to the Westerbork camp in Holland with my wife. We hid our son with a family of friends so he could be saved. Of the rest of my family no one survived: my mother was deported to Sobibor and my brothers to Auschwitz. Inside the camp we were assigned to take care of the orphans. One day a ten year old boy arrived who had been locked up in a small space for one year where he wasn't allowed to speak or move. When he arrived he could only whisper; then all of a sudden he began running incessantly in the courtyard screaming at the top of his lungs. Three days later he was deported to Auschwitz. A few children were saved because of those hiding places but it is impossible to describe the psychological pain inflicted on a child who is forced to live under such conditions for one or two years. The *Diary of Anne Frank* provides some idea:

"In 1944 we were sent to Bergen Belsen camp and a few days later before liberation we were again placed in a freight train going east, which for our good fortune never arrived at its destination: as we were told later on they had prepared the gas chambers at Theresienstadt for us."

In response to a request from Judge Halevy who appears to be following a line of his own to clear up the issue of Jewish collaboration, the witness describes the tasks of the "Councils of Jewish Elders" (Joodenrat) that had also been set up in Holland by the Nazis. "They were to provide the lists of the names to be deported, keep the schools running, publish the proclamations…Inside the

Westerbork camp the Jewish administrators were supposed to provide the names of those to be deported. It was an inhuman task but it did get done. The Jews could have refused to do it but they would have been deported themselves or the people would have been picked at random. In any case it would make no difference at all."

Deputy Prosecutor Bach introduced a number of documents that prove Eichmann's responsibility in the deportations from Belgium and Holland. Servatius wakes up from his passive attitude and approves the introduction into the record of a report showing that Eichmann took the initiative in deporting an entire hospital of mental patients. However, he doesn't accept Eichmann's words: "I shall send a special train to evacuate those sick people to their destination." The difference seems truly inconsequential.

Even in those countries Eichmann didn't mind handling individual cases. To the Foreign Office that was inquiring about a man named Michaelis, Eichmann would answer: "After further examination of the file as a matter of principle I cannot agree to allow the Jew without a country, Michaelis, to emigrate to Switzerland." Here therefore was the person with the power to make a decision! Von Thadden at the Foreign Office had requested that a sympathetic review be made of Mrs. Simmons' file; she was a Jewish woman living with an Italian Catholic and wanted to join him in Italy. But then came September 8, 1943 (the Italian armistice), and Eichmann found another excuse:

> "Following the political changes that have taken place in the meantime I see no reason to discuss the woman's emigration to Italy. I have therefore issued the order to my unit to deport Simmons immediately.
> —(Signed:) Eichmann."

Thursday, May 11

This morning's session was almost entirely dedicated to Italy and once again after the Danish example there was some light shining through the dark clouds that covered Nazi Europe.

"Every Italian Jew owes his life to the Italian population," Fulda Campagnano said, among other things. She is a mathematics teacher who came to testify this morning. She was born in Florence, the daughter of the famous Professor Umberto Cassuto, who used to teach Semitic languages at the University of Rome and later in Jerusalem. Mrs. Campagnano now lives in the Yavne kibbutz. She first discussed the Fascist anti-Semitic laws of 1938. "Italian Jews were excluded from government jobs, from the army, and the professions. However, they were not harmed physically and somehow they managed to find employment. Our freedom and our lives were not in danger. Things changed on September 8, 1943. With the Nazi occupation a different kind of persecution began.

"I was in Florence with my husband and our two children at the time, one was eighteen months old and the other three years old. My brother was the head rabbi of the city. To inform the Jews of Florence of the danger that was threatening them, he went from house to house telling everyone to escape and hide. He also set up a committee to rescue the poorest ones with the help of a Catholic priest whose name I can't remember.

"We used to listen to Radio London at that time and we heard talk of the gas chambers but deep down we thought it was all just propaganda. Italian Jews couldn't believe any such thing could happen to them, perhaps because they had seen that even under Fascism they could go on living.

"By the end of September we went into hiding in a convent with my sister-in-law and the children. My husband stayed to help my brother, who, as the rabbi, refused to abandon his position. On November 27, a Saturday, my husband came to the convent to tell me that the SS had taken my brother while he was holding a meeting with his committee. We went looking for another hiding place that same night and even though the population was ready to help us it became difficult since the Germans had announced that anyone providing any help would be shot. I went from house to house for many days until one evening I waited unsuccessfully for my husband to return to tell me where I could spend the night. I found out later that he and my sister-in-law had an appointment with someone who had promised to help my brother but instead they found the SS waiting for them. My husband was immediately deported to a camp near Auschwitz,

"My brother and sister-in-law were held in the penitentiary in Florence for some time. Then they were both deported. My brother never returned, while my sister-in-law was sent first to Auschwitz then to Theresienstadt, where she was liberated. In 1945 she emigrated to Palestine; three years later she died, killed by the Arabs.

"Alone with six children, my own and my brother's, I again found shelter in a convent. With us there was a woman and her daughter seeking refuge because they were notorious Fascists and they feared the reaction of the partisans. We left the convent because the two women were beginning to suspect that we were Jewish. I received help from a Protestant preacher. One of my children was taken by the Bilour family, who were Protestants, and I am thankful to them that not only was the child saved but that he also kept his mental balance."

Deputy Prosecutor Bach then asked: "Mrs. Campagnano why didn't all the Jews escape, at least after September 8th?"

"I will give you the case of some acquaintances of ours. They didn't move because of the father, who was paralyzed and because of the false sense of security, since one of the daughters had been an active Fascist. She left the house one day to go to the local store and saw how the SS came to drag off her old paralyzed relative, her mother, and her sister.

"The Germans were using lists that had been prepared by the Fascist police. But even the renewal of ration cards was a good opportunity to grab the Jews. One woman went to renew her ration cards with her child and never returned."

Bach: "What do you know about the Jews in Rome?"

Campagnano: "All I know is what I heard after the liberation. In September 1943 the Germans demanded fifty kilos of solid gold in exchange for the safety of the Jews of Rome. The fifty kilos were assembled and delivered. But a few days later the Germans surrounded the entire ghetto, going into each house and bringing out men, women, and children. A few thousand people were deported that way."

Bach: "How do you explain the kind of help you were given?"

Campagnano: "First of all I would like to point out that I was helped not only by the clergy but also by Christian families I didn't even know, from every background, from workers to intellectuals.

There were probably three reasons: the traditional hatred of the Germans, the ongoing struggle for liberation, and the natural kindness of the people. Every Italian Jew owes his life to the Italian people."

With that moving statement Mrs. Campagnano concludes her testimony.

Before and after the witness Deputy Prosecutor Bach introduced a series of documents relating to the Italian chapter that also prove Eichmann's responsibility in that area. On February 24, 1943, the German Foreign Office asked the *Reichführung* of the SS for its requirements regarding the Jewish problem in view of the upcoming conversations between Foreign Minister Ribbentrop and Mussolini. The directives were promised to be ready by the 25th but in the meantime an official at the ministry wrote in his report that "the head of the Reich Security Office is complaining about the negative influence of the Italians that can be felt in Romania, Bulgaria, and Slovakia, where they are beginning to refuse to deport the Jews based on the bad example given by the Italians." The official added a personal comment: "The Italians prevented the restrictions in France and took initiatives favorable to the Jews wherever they could."

The answer bore Müller's signature but, as Eichmann admitted during the pre-trial findings, he had drafted the letter. It describes how Laval and others created obstacles to the German plans against the Jews using the attitude of the Italian government as an excuse.

The German Consul in Rome, Eitel Friedrich Möllhausen, informed the German Foreign Office that Kappler had received orders to deport eight thousand Roman Jews for extermination. In agreement with General Rainer Stahel, the military commander in Rome, he proposed using them to build fortifications instead. But the answer was not long in coming. The Foreign Office, speaking for von Ribbentrop, informed him that due to an order from the Führer the eight thousand Jews in Rome were to be deported to Mauthausen as hostages. Möllhausen was told not to interfere and to let the SS carry out the operation.

In France the Italian consul in Paris petitioned German authorities on April 20, 1943, to avoid the deportation of a Jewish woman, Hasson de Toledo, who had held Italian nationality in the past. Eichmann's deputy in Paris, Roethke, wrote in the margin: "This is all we need now!" One month later the consul again interceded for a Jewish woman from Paris. But the results were the same: both women were to be deported on the first available train.

Eichmann also received a message from von Thadden at the Foreign Office who was relaying the opinion of a top Vatican official advising that it would be best to stop arresting the Jews "under the windows of the Vatican" in order to avoid feeding enemy propaganda and not indispose the Holy See. The office of the defendant also received a request from the singer Toti dal Monte, who had asked the Führer for the freedom of one of her Aryan relatives who had married a Jewish woman. Even in this case the answer remained unchanged: "The address is unknown": a euphemism for death in an extermination camp.

Finally, the prosecution introduced a sworn statement by Colonel Massimo Adolfo Vitale of Rome, according to which 7,496 Jews were deported from Italy and only 610 returned from the concentration camps.

During the morning session one witness, the widow of the rabbi of Oslo, described the deportations of the Norwegian Jews and the generous help that was offered by the local partisans, who were able to bring about half of the Jews into Sweden. In the afternoon the widow of the last president of the Jewish community in Berlin, Mrs. Henschel, testified. Up to the last minute the Nazis took advantage of the organization of the community, whose leaders were forced to collaborate in the deportations.

Friday, May 12

In order to fool world opinion even more easily the Nazis decided to set up a model camp: the ghetto at Theresienstadt near Prague. The leaders of Jewish communities and the most prominent Jews were sent there; but in the end, after some time, all of them reached the gas chambers at Auschwitz.

Today, Mordechai Ansbacher described the conditions inside the camp. He is thirty-four and was deported from the town of Würzburg in Germany with his mother. Ansbacher testified: "At Theresienstadt the German Jews were kept separated from those coming from Czechoslovakia or other countries with whom they carried on endless arguments. But they tried to help one another and often as they were dying of dysentery and hunger and were about to go scavenging on potato peels, they would say: 'Excuse me, doctor. You were ahead of me. Excuse me…' Many thought they could save themselves because of their past services: some were severely wounded veterans, others were large landowners, others still were university professors.

"I was sixteen at the time and the younger people were under the guidance of two men who were teaching us about Zionism, organizing ceremonies for the religious holidays, and encouraging us to help the older folks. The camp enjoyed a semblance of autonomy because of a 'Council of Elders,' presided over by Edelstein, who was also deported to Auschwitz. But dysentery and typhus were rampant and the lack of water and food, coupled with the awful sanitary conditions, would all quickly have lethal consequences.

"One day they told us we were to leave to build a new camp in another town. The older people bade us farewell with the following words: 'We are proud of you because you shall finish building what we were unable to complete here.' I also had illusions. I managed to send a ticket to my mother begging her to come with me. She was able to get on a train. But her destination was Auschwitz and she died there.

"In 1944 a Red Cross team arrived. A curfew was imposed on part of the barracks and only those who still looked human were allowed to go outside. Some houses were whitewashed and a few signs were posted outside: 'Central School,' 'Ghetto Theater.' For the children they rushed to build a small glass palace with painted tiny beds and blankets embroidered with hearts. The children had to go through many rehearsals to make sure everything was working properly and on those occasions they would be fed. The elders then took advantage of the situation, sending different children each time to allow each one to have some food." The witness has finished his testimony and there was no further doubt that the Nazis were the masters of the elaborate cover-up! Among the documents introduced by the prosecution, some were proof of Eichmann's connection to the Würzburg deportations, the witness's hometown, while others indicated how he was present at all the meetings that combined various ministries having to do with anti-Jewish measures. During one of those meetings as it appears in the minutes, Dr. Hans Globke, who is currently part of Konrad Adenauer's staff, was also present.

Monday, May 15

Today the court heard only one witness, Justice Michael Mus-manno of the Supreme Court of Pennsylvania. Defense attorney Serva-tius had opposed the introduction of the witness because he had been one of the judges at the Nuremberg trial and the principle of the *res judicata* did not allow him to testify. However, the court agreed to allow Musmanno's testimony limiting it to his conversations with Nazi leaders who were already dead. The witness had been asked by the U.S. Navy to conduct an investigation into Hitler's death, which gave him the opportunity to come into contact with the top Nazi leadership.

Musmanno told the court what those Nazi officials thought of the defendant. Göring was the most forthcoming, stating that Eichmann had full power regarding the extermination of the Jews. Ribbentrop went so far as saying that Eichmann was even influencing Hitler himself, who had made a mistake in concentrating such vast power in Eichmann's hands. Hans Frank, the governor of Poland, asked Himmler to put an end to the massacre of the Jews but was told to go to Eichmann, who rejected the idea. General Karl Kohler of the Luftwaffe told the witness how during the closing days of the war he had argued with Hitler about the order to shoot captured enemy pilots. Kohler refused to carry out the order but Eichmann kept insisting that they should shoot all the Jewish flyers.

Walter Schellenberg, another Nazi official, who headed the secret service and was very close to Hitler, told Musmanno that for some time Eichmann worked entirely on his own. This happened between Heydrich's death when he was head of the Reich Security Services, and the appointment of his successor, Ernst Kaltenbrunner. The fact that he was only a lieutenant colonel didn't prevent Eichmann from carrying out his plans, since he could always use Hitler's name.

Schellenberg also provided more details to the witness concerning the infamous *Einsatzgruppen* assigned to murder the Jews. Even though officially their task was to protect the rear, they were not actually fighting units: in effect they were murderers in uniform. The officers were appointed by Himmler upon Eichmann's recommendation. Whoever requested it could be exempt from taking part in those groups to avoid lowering the morale of the others.

For the first time the defense attorney frequently used his prerogative to cross examine the witness. Servatius attempted to discredit the Nazi leaders on several occasions because according to him they were attempting to save themselves by accusing someone else. The witness replied: "But none of them avoided the sentence and furthermore why did they all name Eichmann as the most important man in the extermination of the Jews and not Müller, for example, who was of much higher rank?"

Tuesday, May 16

Today Dr. Heinrich Gruber, a Protestant Reverend from Berlin, who risked his life to save Jews and was deported to Dachau, testified about his meetings with Eichmann. His testimony made a strong impression on the judges and the public.

In order to organize Jewish emigration, Dr. Gruber, with the agreement of Leo Baeck, the Chief Rabbi of Berlin, had several meetings with the leaders of the Gestapo and with the defendant. "I have not come here motivated by hatred or revenge, but I must say that Eichmann appeared to be like a block of ice or marble, devoid of any kind of human feelings. I was never to leave his office with a positive response. He never said that he would have to consult his superiors: he gave the impression of having full power. At that time I couldn't conceive how a human being could act that way and commit such crimes with so much cruelty." The witness then told how some members of the Gestapo helped him at times and cited the example of von Rath, the father of the councilor at the legation killed in Paris in 1938 by a young Jewish man. The witness didn't wish to reveal the name of a second Gestapo officer who often helped him in his humanitarian efforts.

When the court asked him to explain his reticence, Dr. Gruber answered: "This person has an important position today. Given the situation in Germany at this time, I cannot cite his name without his authorization. I have also received a stack of threatening letters; they make no impression upon me but I don't want others to be harmed." The mysterious Gestapo officer was tried by the Polish authorities along with other Nazis but he was later freed because of the testimony by the current witness and by Poland's president. "If some were generous in giving help, many Germans lacked any civic courage. As, for example, the general in charge of the Stettin military district, who asked me to take steps to save some Jews but did nothing himself."

To questions by the prosecutor about his suffering in Dachau concentration camp, the witness chose not to respond. "They knocked out all my teeth," he said. "I developed a heart condition. But my pains cannot compare to those of my Jewish friends. It's impossible to imagine what took place, since where the greatest cruelty was to take place there were no witnesses or documents. In Dante's inferno you could at least scream and cry, but that wasn't even allowed in the death camps."

The witness then cited the mass deportations of priests and clergymen in Germany, Holland, Yugoslavia, and other countries.

In discussing the cooperation with Catholic bishops the witness recalled the help offered by Pope Pius XI, whom he was to meet just before the war broke out. "Few countries were ready to help. The doors of the foreign embassies in Berlin were closed to us."

With his voice shaking from emotion, while his wife and two children accompany him for the trip and listen to his words, visibly moved, Dr. Gruber asks to make a personal statement: "I am the first German to appear before this court and this is very difficult for me. I hope that what I said will help all humanity and not just better understanding between Germany and Israel. My hope is that the universal forgiveness of love shall extend to the defendant and that evil shall be forgiven by God."

Mrs. Carlotta Salzberger was the final witness during the afternoon session. She was deported to Theresienstadt and summoned to the camp headquarters where she met Eichmann and other SS officers. Defense attorney Servatius had asked, during the morning, for the questioning of Herbert Kappler, who was responsible for the Ardeatine massacre and currently held in the penitentiary at Gaeta. The prosecutor announced this evening that he already took the necessary steps with the Italian authorities.

Wednesday, May 17

During the only session of the day the court examined some 80 documents introduced by the prosecution, without any witnesses being called to testify. This was therefore a more relaxed day, following the high point of emotion felt yesterday when Reverend Gruber made his appeal for forgiveness. Eichmann, on the other hand, who shows the greatest interest whenever documents are displayed, was quite active in taking notes.

In their cold bureaucratic language studded with acronyms, these documents allow us to uncover the secrets of the Gestapo's organization and establish the defendant's precise position within the Nazi hierarchy.

The documents refer to every kind of subject. The relations between the Gestapo and the Foreign Office, for example: the 1941 agreement between von Ribbentrop and Himmler regarding actions against Jews of foreign nationality or administrative issues that had to be decided in order to confiscate Jewish possessions and divide the spoils or to pay for the transportation costs for the deportations. As a sick joke to top things off, those expenses were charged as special contributions made by the deportees themselves.

Eichmann's signature appears with increasing frequency on the letters of the IV B4 section he headed. He managed to find the time to personally oversee the deportation to the east of individual Jews: as in the case of the aging Alfred Phillipson, who was not allowed to die peacefully in his own home in spite of the intervention of the Swedish representative. Eichmann gave the orders to confiscate the possessions, works of art, and the property belonging to the Jews. When in 1942 the Italian embassy requested that the apartment belonging to Countess Socconi in Magdeburg not be subject to confiscation, the German Foreign Ministry referred the issue to Eichmann.

But a much more precise assessment of the defendant's prerogatives is available from the minutes of a meeting at the RSHA that took place on March 6, 1942, and was chaired by Eichmann. On that occasion he announced the deportation of 50,000 Jews from Austria and Moravia and asked his officers to strictly follow his instructions, keeping the action absolutely secret so that the Jews would have no inkling of their impending fate.

When the German Foreign Office felt it was expedient to keep some 30,000 Jews, who were foreign nationals, in special camps to be held for future exchanges, the decision was Eichmann's to make.

One after another the judges received deportation orders, scrupulously detailed reports regarding personal possessions that had been confiscated from the prisoners, and the instructions given to the police to provide escorts for the freight trains that brought the Jews to the death camps in the east, one thousand at a time.

Thursday, May 18

The documents and the testimony of today's session are mostly about the model ghetto at Theresienstadt, the only camp the Red Cross was allowed to visit. Of the greatest interest among the documents introduced by the prosecution are the depositions of Siegfried Seidl and Karl Rahm, the first and last Theresienstadt camp commandants, respectively. Both mention the frequent visits by Eichmann to the camp and the orders he gave, including punishing with death anyone attempting to send mail to the outside world. Paul Dunant, the representative of the International Red Cross who visited the ghetto in 1944, recalled his many meetings with Eichmann, who admitted having played a leading role in organizing the Auschwitz and Lublin camps. Those documents show how Eichmann would often come to the model ghetto and get involved in minute details of what was happening inside.

Witeslav Diamant, an electrician who now lives in Herzlia near Tel Aviv, told the court about his experience at Theresienstadt, where, placing his life at risk, he kept a secret copy of the ghetto's register of deaths and births. "One day," he said," I was summoned to camp headquarters. I had to face a commission of ten SS officers. I was told later on that the one seated in the center was Eichmann. But I wouldn't be able to recognize him today. Someone was taking notes next to each name. That evening one of our council members who was present at the meeting told me: 'You will live—next to your name they made a small circle. My two brothers instead must die—there was a cross next to their names.'"

Then Adolf Engelstein, an engineer, took the stand. He also lives in Herzlia and was sent early in 1944, along with other Theresienstadt internees, to the village of Zossen near Berlin. An SS officer, *Obersturmbannführer* Eichmann, was on hand to welcome them and tell them what to do. For about one year some 200 prisoners, often replaced by new ones, were building some 40 huts hidden in the forest that were meant to serve as offices of the Gestapo. Another underground construction in reinforced concrete was, according to the rumors that were circulating, to serve as Hitler's personal shelter.

Back at Theresienstadt in 1945 Engelstein was given a new task. "We were to shut down all the openings of an older building. They said it was to be a warehouse for vegetables. One day, special doors arrived and written on them was: 'Gas proof.' We then understood that we were building gas chambers."

Ernst Recht, a third witness, told the court about the Prague warehouses, where the possessions of the Jews were being collected: in 1943 they included 44,000 rugs and one million books. Günther, Eichmann's personal representative in Prague, wanted to keep the most unusual pieces for himself.

Friday, May 19

In Yugoslavia as well the attitude of the Italian authorities toward the Jews was different from that of the Nazis: this clearly appears in the testimony of the witnesses and even more from the documents introduced today by the prosecutor. At the start of the afternoon session, the only one held today, Dr. Hinko Salz from Tel Aviv was the first to take the stand. He was a medical officer in the Yugoslav army. Taken prisoner a few days after the war broke out, Dr. Salz first worked as liaison in a military hospital. His father who was over seventy, died at that time due to the bad treatment he received in the work detail he had been assigned to. A few months later, in July 1941, 1500 Jews in Belgrade were ordered to appear in a city square the following day or face the death penalty. The witness was part of a group of 100 Jewish hostages who were to be shot if a 17 year old who was accused of sabotage was not given up by the community. "I understood that this was a desperate situation," said the witness. "I took a step forward and waved the travel document issued to me by the hospital as I said as authoritatively as I could: 'I protest on the basis of the Geneva Convention; I am an officer and a prisoner of war.' The SS commander looked at me and with one wave of the hand ordered that I be set free."

A few days later the witness managed to reach the Italian zone of occupation and safety. From Ljubliana he went to Italy and then on to Switzerland.

The second witness of the day, Alexander Arnon, was also saved by the Italian authorities. He was the secretary of the Jewish community in Zagreb and in that capacity he visited the concentration camps in Croatia where the Ustashi, Ante Pavelic's fascists, killed tens of thousands of Serbs, Jews, and gypsies. When the Jadovna camp was about to be taken over by Italian troops the Ustashi were speeding up the shootings. Of the 75,000 Jews living in Yugoslavia before the war, the Nazis and the Croatians killed 60,000. "Unfortunately, no one protested. The Catholic Church in Croatia didn't utter a word of protest against the deportation of the Jews."

The witness managed to escape to Ljubljana, then occupied by Italian troops. "While I was in the hospital they handed me the extradition order. When I went to the Italian police a few days later the commissioner told me that they made sure they had lost the file and I was able to stay. I was sent to an assigned residence in the village of

Alba in the province of Cuneo. After September 8, I was saved by a peasant family and then escaped into Switzerland."

Some of the documents introduced today refer to the Italian authorities. "In Dubrovnik," one reads in a report sent to the German Foreign Office, "the Italians have allowed the Jews to remain in town and stay in the hotels assigned to the German troops; at Mostar the Italian Chief of Staff is opposing the deportations and said that the Italian army was not going to demean itself by taking measures against the Jews, since the entire civilian population was to be subjected to the same laws." According to another German Foreign Office document an Italian officer had replied to German pressure by saying, "The anti-Semitic measures are incompatible with the honor of the army."

Monday, May 22

At the start of the afternoon session, the only one to be held today, prosecutor Gideon Hausner told the court that he had secured Eich-mann's original memoirs, the same ones previously published by *Life* magazine. It is the transcription of sixty tapes, almost as many as Eich-mann recorded in his Israeli jail when he was questioned. The prosecu-tor also stated that in view of the agreements between Italy and Israel, Herbert Kappler, the former Nazi police chief in Rome and now in the military penitentiary at Gaeta, will be questioned in Italy.

The prosecution then completed the documentation on the exter-mination of the Croatian Jews. The efforts by the Italian embassy to save a Jewish woman from Zagreb from being deported to Auschwitz, and those by the Vatican to obtain the emigration of 400 Jews to Palestine, were all stopped by Eichmann's office. After September 8, 1943, a special group was set up under the leadership of Hermann Krumey, one of Eichmann's close collaborators, to deport the Jews out of the area where until then they had been given Italian protection.

To complete the picture of the persecutions in the Balkans Hausner introduced a set of documents on Greece.

The difference in the Italian attitude is again obvious from a long exchange of letters between the German Foreign Office and Eich-mann's department.

The Italian embassy in Berlin presented a formal protest because of the interference of Wisliceny in the Italian zone of occupation and because of the inclusion of Italian Jews among those deported from Salonica to Poland. In 1943 Eichmann had sent Wisliceny to Greece to deport 54,000 Jews residing in Salonica. Only 1,900 were to return from the death camps.

In March 1943 von Mackensen, the German ambassador to Rome, was informed that the Italian Foreign Ministry was refusing to hasten the deportation by stripping the Jews of their citizenship.

Other documents describe the measures taken by the SS with the agreement of Max Merten, the military commander in Salonica. The progression followed a well-rehearsed pattern: first came the obligation to wear the yellow star, then the ghettos were set up—as well as forced labor—and then finally came the deportations. Wisliceny wanted them interrupted because of the epidemics that were rampant among the Jews, but Eichmann ordered that they be resumed immediately and that's what happened.

Then Izhak Nehama took the stand, the only survivor of a family of ten deported to Auschwitz. He tells how on one Saturday 9,000 Jews were assembled in a square in Salonica. The prosecutor showed the witness a few pictures taken on that occasion. When he looked at the last photograph the witness was amazed for a moment, then he said: "Yes that's me! It was two in the afternoon and since six in the morning I had to keep flexing in front of an SS thug. And how many times I got hit! What had I ever done to him?"

The colorful language used by the witness, a simple man, has the audience smiling even though the subject is far from being funny.

Tuesday, May 23

Today the court examined documents and heard testimony about Nazi persecution in Romania and Slovakia.

Mrs. Perla Mark told the story of how her husband, the head rabbi of Chernowitz, was caught by the SS in July 1941 and forced to watch the burning of his synagogue and the rolls of the Laws kept inside, before being shot on the banks of the river Prut. Mrs. Mark explained:

"Most of the 70,000 Jews of Chernowitz were deported to Transnistria, where they died. My father and mother slipped and fell along the road and were shot then and there. My son, who was a medical student in Prague, was sent to Auschwitz where he was forced to play the cello in the orchestra that welcomed the deportees to the camp. He went on playing until 1944, until he too ended up in the gas chamber.

Then Theodore Loewenstein took the stand. He used to teach Jewish history at Bucharest. "In a few months in 1941 in Bessarabia 160,000 Jews were massacred. Across all of Romania they reached 300,000. During a pogrom organized by the Iron Guard 125 Jews were hanged on meat hooks with a sign that read "Kosher meat" (butchered according to the Jewish custom). At first, the local government collaborated with the Nazis, but later it allowed the emigration to Palestine of a few thousand people. The ambassadors of neutral countries approached General Ion Antonescu: Sweden, Switzerland, Turkey, as well as the Apostolic Nunzio Monsignor Umberto Casullo, who also provided funds collected by the Holy See. Among the documents introduced there is a letter addressed to Eichmann from his deputy in Romania, Gustav Richter, regarding the sailing of the ship *Struma* for Palestine. Turkish authorities forced the ship to turn back into the Black Sea where it was sunk with over 700 Jews on board.

Another document shows that Eichmann, having found out that over one thousand Jewish children were about to emigrate from Romania to Palestine, asked the Foreign Office to prevent any such emigration by any and all means available.

Regarding Slovakia we heard the testimony of Dr. Ernst Abeles, one of the heads of the Jewish community of Bratislava. The witness described the initial anti-Semitic legislation in Slovakia and the arrival of Wisliceny, Eichmann's deputy. He recalled: "One day I was summoned to the offices of the Jewish center. I found Eichmann next to Wisliceny, who scolded me for spending too much money in assisting needy families, according to the numbers he was looking at. He then ordered me to shut down the Palestinian office which I was in charge of. I remember his words but I honestly would not be able to recognize him today."

The witness then described the rescue attempts made by the Jewish committee he was part of and that was headed by a brave woman: Gisi Fleishmann, who would later be deported to Auschwitz. After paying 40 to 50,000 dollars, she managed to get Wisliceny to interrupt the deportations and have a period of relative calm. They even discussed the possible end of all deportations in Europe for the payment of two to three million dollars. Wisliceny appeared to be close to agreeing to the deal, excluding Poland where, he said, the Jews were already lost. But the matter was not pursued. The witness also recalled his meetings with Brünner, the Szered camp commandant, who with a brief movement of his cane decided which Jew would go to work and which one would die. Brünner was also the one who promised the representative of the International Red Cross, Dunant, to allow foreign Jews to emigrate, since most of them were from South America. But he demanded that they all be assembled in a single location at Marienka where a special train would take them to Switzerland.

Hundreds of Jews came out of their hiding places. But the train that left Marienka took them to Auschwitz and the gas chambers instead.

In a letter to the German Foreign Office Eichmann wrote that a proposed exchange of 5,000 Jewish children for 20,000 Germans would soon become impossible for "technical reasons."

Among the documents introduced by the prosecution for Slovakia there is also the important and well-known deposition by Wisliceny, where he states how deportation orders arrived sent by cable by Eichmann.

Wednesday, May 24

The prosecution has set aside for a few hours the matter of the Nazi persecution of Slovakian Jews to introduce a large number of documents on another crime that the defendant is accused of having committed: the murder of the children in the Czech village of Lidice. Reinhard Heydrich, Eichmann's direct superior, was assassinated in an attack in Prague in 1942 and as a reprisal the order was issued to deport all the children from the village of Lidice. Some 88 children then arrived at Lodz and Hermann Krumey, head of the Jewish emigration office, asked Eichmann for instructions. "I am asking department IV-B-4 because I assume these children must be given special treatment." Whenever special treatment was mentioned, since it was a well-known bureaucratic euphemism for murder, it had to go to Eichmann for approval.

The defendant was also involved in propaganda. Even Dr. Tuka, the head of the Slovak collaborationist government, insisted on visiting the concentration camps because he had heard rumors that they were actually death camps. Eichmann then invited a Slovak journalist, Fritz Fiala, who was an honorary member of the Gestapo, to visit a *lager*, without letting him see the crematoriums or the gas chambers and having him write articles filled with praise, which he then sent to Dr. Tuka.

The court overruled the objections of the defense and accepted the introduction of the long report compiled by Dr. Rudolf Kastner after the liberation. Dr. Kastner had dealt personally with Eichmann in Budapest and he will be discussed at length in the days to come: his is the greatest absence at this trial—he was killed for political reasons few years ago.

The courtroom is filled today by a crowd eager to hear the truth about Rudolf Kastner's dealings with the Nazis. Many people can remember when, on the night of March 4, 1957, three shots tragically ended his life. He was probably the most controversial Israeli citizen of the postwar period, and the editor of a Hungarian language daily, *Ujkelet,* when he was shot in the back one night in Tel Aviv by a few young men who quickly escaped in a big black car. Ten days later he died without having regained consciousness.

During the Nazi occupation, Kastner was the president of the Hungarian Zionist Federation, part of the world Zionist movement, with its leadership in Palestine. In order to save the Hungarian Jews from being killed, he attempted the most dangerous path of holding negotiations directly with the Nazis, and with Eichmann in particular. About 1650 managed to save their own lives but the overwhelming majority of the Hungarian Jews were murdered anyway.

After the end of the war some people in Israel accused Kastner of collaborating and he retaliated by bringing actions in court for defamation. But the court, then presided by the same Benjamin Halevy who is now judging the Eichmann case, decided the case against Kastner and stated in his judgment that he, Kastner, "had sold his soul to the devil." The judgment that also reflected badly on the Zionist leaders who now head the State of Israel caused a government crisis and was the object of long debates.

A few years later the tragic consequence of the verdict would be Kastner's murder. Today, only parts of his report were being quoted regarding Slovakia and the rescue operation by Mrs. Gisi Fleishmann, who died at Auschwitz for refusing to stop her work. Adolf Rosenberg testified about the Szered camp in Slovakia. He was a carpenter at the camp and was able to avoid deportation to the gas chambers on two occasions. The first time in October 1944 he passed by Brünner, the camp commandant, who with a wave of his hand sent him to the right and to his death. "When I reached the SS, I went to the left, with those staying in the camp. They yelled at me 'Where are you going?' But I just kept on walking and they let me go. I am unable to explain this. A second time a few days later, I was already scheduled to leave for Auschwitz with my parents when I heard someone calling me one night. One of the SS guards in the commando gave me a military cap and a safe conduct saying: 'Go quickly, run away.' I hid in the cellar of the carpenter's barracks and saved my life a second time."

After Slovakia it was Hungary's turn. Without a doubt this is one of the keys of the prosecution's case since Eichmann was personally in charge in Hungary and no longer giving orders from his Berlin office as he had mostly been doing so far. The defendant's actions began after March 19, 1944, when German troops invaded Hungary.

We shall summarize that part of the Public Prosecutor's presentation.

The Extermination of the Hungarian Jews

In 1944 Hungary, with its 800,000 Jews, was the only country within the Nazi sphere of influence with a large Jewish population.

Since 1942 the Nazis were applying constant pressure on the Hungarian government to adopt anti-Semitic laws but the Magyars had limited themselves only to denying the Jews some rights.

In April 1943 the Regent, Admiral Horthy, was invited to attend a meeting with Hitler and Ribbentrop, who told him that there were only two possibilities: either lock up the Jews in concentration camps or exterminate them. Horthy, however, was not convinced. He was then called to another meeting with Hitler on March 17, 1944, and while he was reading the ultimatum he had been handed, German troops were occupying all of Hungary without firing a shot. Behind the army came Eichmann with his special unit: the fate of the Hungarian Jews was sealed. He had to work quickly because the Soviets were getting closer, so there was a sense of urgency in the actions taken by the defendant and his assistants, a desire to "complete" their work at all costs. Later on when the collaborator Ferenc Szálasi was appointed prime minister, Eichmann could also count on the Hungarian administration to further his own ends.

In Budapest he was no longer simply the director, the planner pulling the strings from afar; he was acting actually as an independent executor, Himmler's plenipotentiary representative who could count on the full cooperation of Lazlo Endre, the Hungarian secretary of state for Jewish Affairs.

The lesson of the Warsaw ghetto had not been lost on the head of *Amt* IV B4, who was determined to prevent such an episode from happening again. Orders were sent to Rudolf Höss to immediately reactivate the Auschwitz installations. The camp commandant traveled to Budapest to coordinate the deportations with Eichmann, who was insisting on frequent transports that Höss claimed to be unable to accommodate. They finally reached an agreement and Auschwitz had never seen an active period such as the summer and fall of 1944.

The gas chambers and crematoria were working day and night and at times 10,000 Jews were being killed daily.

On March 20, 1944, the day after the occupation, Wisliceny and Krumey, Eichmann's main lieutenants, summoned the leaders of the Jewish community to announce the formation of a new council under

Nazi control. The defendant, as head of the *Sondereinsatz-Kommando Eichmann,* was now the absolute master of the Hungarian Jews.

Massive deportations began in mid-May 1944. The details and the various phases of the operation were prepared by Eichmann. At the same time he began discussions with Rudolf Kastner and Joel Brand. In exchange for trucks, coffee, tea, and soap the Germans would save thousands of Jews and agreed to undertake with the Allies not to use the trucks on the Western front. Minister of Foreign Affairs Ribbentrop, having heard the news of the deal from London radio, gave instructions to Ambassador Veesenmayer in Budapest to prevent it. In the meantime Kurt Becher, a high official in the SS, was entering into talks in Himmler's name and to ease the negotiations he was able to send a train with 1684 Jews to Bergen Belsen, then to Switzerland after payment of $1,000 per person.

According to a high SS official, Walter Schellenberg, Himmler wanted to improve his reputation and be accepted by the Allies as the negotiator of a future armistice.

But Eichmann began the massive deportations the day after Brand left for Turkey where he was to contact Allied emissaries. The fury of the SS colonel was focused against a young Swedish architect, Raul Wallenberg, who was using his diplomatic immunity to save as many Jews as he could. Tens of thousands owe him their lives and his initiatives awaken a sad thought: how many more in Europe could have been saved had there been a few more people like him.

The deportations took place in total secrecy. The Red Army was advancing. Up until the end of June, according to an official German report, 437,000 Hungarian Jews were deported to the death camps.

Thanks to Horthy's action the plan to deport all the Jews in Budapest in a single day was never enacted.

Horthy, unwilling to continue to fight alongside the Germans, was overthrown on October 15, 1944, and Ferenc Szálasi, head of the Arrow Cross, took power. Eichmann, who had previously left Budapest when Horthy had opposed the continued deportations, suddenly returned. There were no more trains. Himmler had ordered that the extermination be interrupted. But Eichmann got around the orders and organized the tragic "march on foot" to Vienna, two hundred kilometers away, in the dead of winter. The corpses were piling up on the sides of the road. Even Himmler reprimanded Eichmann for that decision and the march was stopped. The other Jews in Budapest were liberated by the Red Army.

This evening Pinchas Freudiger, head of the orthodox Jewish community of Budapest, testified.

He told the court how years before he had helped the Jews of Bratislava, giving them part of the money that was given to Wisliceny to stop the deportations. Therefore, after the occupation began and the representatives of the Jews of Budapest were summoned to a meeting attended by Wisliceny, the witness was one of the few who understood what was in store for them in spite of what Krumey, the other Eichmann deputy, was telling them, urging them to remain calm.

Thursday, May 25

Two incidents this morning forced Judge Landau to interrupt the hearing for the first time since the trial began. He also announced that if there were other incidents he would be compelled to close the courtroom to the public, allowing only the journalists to remain.

The first incident took place during the testimony of Pinchas Freudiger regarding the deportation of the Hungarian Jews. A man in his fifties got up in the courtroom and addressed the witness in Hungarian saying: "You sent tranquillizer injections to the ghetto so that people wouldn't escape. You said we shouldn't worry!" Then right after that an old man began insulting the witness in Yiddish and Judge Landau had to interrupt the hearing. Suddenly it seemed that instead of the trial of Adolf Eichmann it was about to become the trial of Jewish collaborators. The judge in the Kastner trial, Benjamin Halevy, seems intent on shedding light on that page of history.

Six witnesses heard today recalled some aspect of the persecutions in Hungary. Freudiger, who had started his testimony yesterday, was called in by Wisliceny one day and heard a proposal to save the Jews based on one large payment in dollars as had taken place in Slovakia. Krumey, another close collaborator of Eichmann, received $220,000: the preamble to the famous Jews-for-trucks deal that the witness had nothing to do with and we certainly can expect to hear about during the next sessions. Eichmann told the witness in April 1944 that he had given the order to lock up in ghettos 300,000 Hungarian Jews living in the so-called border areas. They were actually deported to the gas chambers. The initiatives by Franklin D. Roosevelt and the king of Sweden to Admiral Horthy stopped the deportations out of Budapest, and the 200,000 Jews living in the capital were saved for the most part. Later on, following advice from Wisliceny, the witness fled to Romania with his family to avoid Eichmann's wrath.

Elisheva Senesz testifies that already in 1943 she had heard that the Jews were being killed at Auschwitz. When she told one of the Jewish leaders, he answered: "You are a great woman poet and truly have a great imagination." But a few months later she was deported to Auschwitz herself and her words turned out to be the truth.

Mardit Reich, a frail seventy-year-old woman showed the court the photocopy of a postcard and a letter that her husband threw out of a train and that someone mailed back to her. He wrote, among other things: "Dearest wife and children. May the hand that mails this letter be blessed. We are leaving on a long trip. May God protect you. Perhaps a miracle will happen and I will return. I hug you. Your father from the freight train, Thursday about eleven." The witness has to stop reading because she is crying and many in the audience are also emotional. Eichmann shows no reaction.

Zeew Sapir was deported to Auschwitz with his parents and brothers and then sent to work at another location with 200 other Jews. Exhausted by the march and fasting for three days, they could no longer walk. They were ordered to dig their pit. Then they were taken to a mess hall where a huge pot was set in the center of the room. But the pot was empty. An SS officer had them come closer and shot them one by one with a bullet in the back of the head at the edge of the pot. Only 11 were able to escape the massacre. The witness was able to escape into the forest after another execution by shooting and two days later he was saved by the Red Army.

By his questions Servatius tried to confirm the defense thesis that the Hungarian gendarmes were responsible for the actual deportations and not Eichmann's agents.

Matti Foeldi, a lawyer from Uzhorod in Carpathian Russia, testified how he too was deported to Auschwitz with his wife and two children. "When we arrived," he stated, "they had us get out of the freight cars very quickly and they separated us. Women and children on the left, and the men on the right. I could recognize my daughter from a distance because she was wearing a red overcoat. In the crowd I could follow that red dot that became smaller. Then nothing more."

Friday, May 26

The idealized description of Eichmann as the cold executor of orders coming from higher up but personally removed from the killers themselves, was seriously challenged today. According to one witness he killed a young Hungarian Jewish boy with his own hands. Avraham Gordon was sent to work in a suburb of Budapest with a group of young Jews. They were to dig some trenches in the garden of the villa that Eichmann had requisitioned. One day Eichmann's driver grabbed one of the boys, who had to be about sixteen, and cried out: "You stole cherries from the tree!" and locked him up in a tool shed. "Later on," said the witness, "I saw the driver go into the shed with Eichmann. The boy inside began crying, begging, and screaming for some fifteen minutes. Then the cries stopped and Eichmann came out. He was out of breath with traces of fresh blood on his shirt, he was mumbling: 'Useless people…'" Later on the driver and an SS guard dragged the body of the boy and placed it on an amphibious car. On his way back the driver told us: "I threw that stinking body in the Danube. You will also end up that way."

Dr. Tibor Ferencz, as deputy people's prosecutor in Hungary after the liberation, met a few war criminals, László Endre and László Baky among them. "I saw them for one hour before they were hanged, when they knew they were going to die. Endre, who had been Deputy Minister of the Interior and Commissioner of Jewish Affairs, told me that orders regarding the Jews came from Eichmann and that he passed them on to be implemented to Baky, the head of the Hungarian gendarmerie. Eichmann had given Endre a dressing down several times because the deportations were not proceeding at the desired pace and he had complained to the Hungarian Interior Minister Andor Jaross. But Jaross answered: "What can I do? They are the masters!"

The prosecutor introduced various documents received from the Hungarian government, among them the records of a meeting of the heads of Jewish organizations that was held in Budapest with Eichmann, Krumey, and Wisliceny in March 1944, the same one mentioned by the witness Freudiger yesterday. Eichmann suggested that they put an end to the democratic methods of their coreligionists and he promised to defend the Jews and their property if they scrupulously followed his directives.

Another document mentions contacts with the Regent Horthy to stop the deportations. Eichmann was against it and appealed to Himmler, who chose to delay any decision. On the other hand given the military situation, without the collaboration of the Hungarians the deportations became impossible.

Monday, May 29

At times imitating Eichmann's metallic voice and often stopped by his emotions, Joel Brand, the most important witness to testify at this trial, told the court today about the "blood for supplies" negotiations. In his glass booth Eichmann lost the mask of detached indifference he usually wore during other testimony and penned some lengthy notes to his defense attorney. We may find out about their content tomorrow when Servatius can cross examine the witness.

Rather short, stout and fair haired with a pale complexion, Brand, who was a mysterious adventurer, now looks more like a good family man. His activity as one of the leaders of the Zionist organization in Budapest began in 1941 when stateless Jews were first being deported to Poland. Hungary was occupied by the Nazis on March 19, 1944. Brand and his comrades managed to bring 20,000 Jews into Hungary, illegally saving them from the countries where the massacres were already underway. Thanks to these refugees the Brand group could draw an accurate picture of the situation in the ghettos and camps, even in remote locations. That information was immediately forwarded to Switzerland and Turkey. The rescue operation was set up by a committee called *waada*, chaired by Kastner, with Samuel Springmann and Brand himself. Agents of Hungarian and German counterespionage of the Canaris group played the role of couriers and ensured communications with Switzerland and Turkey. When it found out that Wisliceny was part of the Eichmann group, the committee met with him and paid him 200,000 dollars in various installments. In exchange they obtained the freedom of a few Jews who had been arrested and were allowed to visit some camps.

The witness then recalled his four meetings with the defendant. The first time Eichmann, wearing his tailored SS uniform, said: "Do you realize who I am? I am in charge of the entire action. Now it's Hungary's turn. I am ready to trade one million Jews for supplies. You choose!" he screamed. "Supplies or blood, blood or supplies? I am an idealistic German and you are an idealistic Jew with whom we can talk at the same table. But perhaps tomorrow we will meet on the battlefield. So now you must decide quickly: in which country do you wish to go to hold the negotiations?"

As Brand recalls: "At that time I was both happy and sad all at once: we were holding a very big card in our hands. Eichmann asked me to keep the secret from the Hungarian authorities and to talk only to my friends. The committee made a unanimous decision to try and send me to Constantinople where there was an office of the Jewish Agency.

A few days later Eichmann called me in once more. He was holding a packet of letters and a large amount of money in foreign currency. "Here," he said, "this came in for you through your secret courier. You can censor the letters. I have no time for that!"

It was clear that Klages of the SS espionage service, who was present at that meeting, was very much interested in the success of those negotiations. He had pressured Eichmann to hand over the money to us and avoid burning our bridges to the outside world.

"At our last meeting," said Brand, "Eichmann was screaming once again because I hadn't yet left. Krumey then gave me the necessary documents. The proposal was clear: one million Jews for 100,000 trucks that would be deployed only on the Russian front and perhaps also a few tons of coffee, tea, and soap. My wife and children were to stay in Hungary as hostages. It was May 15, 1944. Eichmann told me that the deportations to the tune of 12,000 Jews daily were to begin the same day. He added that I had the power to avoid all this. If I came back with a positive answer, he would blow up the installations at Auschwitz and would take the first 10,000 Jews to a border of our choosing to receive a consignment of 1000 trucks only afterward. The following day Krumey took me to Vienna and put me on a plane to Istanbul. Just before take off he said: "Tell your friends abroad that not all SS officers are like Eichmann…some of them are honest like Wisliceny and myself."

So Brand left for Turkey with that load of human lives to bear that still weighs heavily on his shoulders today. His testimony will continue tomorrow.

Before he took the stand American psychologist Gustave Gilbert testified that he had visited the Nuremberg criminals in their cells. Among other things he gave the court a diary and unpublished auto-biography of Rudolf Höss, the Auschwitz commandant where Eich-mann is mentioned several times as being in charge of the action to exterminate the Jews. The psychiatrist stated: "They all said that the orders came from Hitler, but agreed that Eichmann was the main executor of those orders."

Tuesday, May 30

The transaction of "supplies for blood" that we heard about yester-day was the focal point of today's two hearings. Joel Brand continued with his testimony. Once he reached Constantinople with the passport provided by Eichmann, he was to travel on to Aleppo to meet with Moshe Shertok, one of the heads of the Jewish Agency. But at the Syrian border Brand was arrested by the British military authorities who took him to a jail in Cairo. It was in vain that Brand told Shertok that it was imperative they should obtain at least a delay, even some fictitious agreement, if thousands of lives were not to be lost. The Jewish Agency was powerless. The prosecution revealed this today with a series of documents of extraordinary interest that remained un-published and constitute a heavy indictment of England and its allies.

Shertok requested that Brand be allowed to return to Hungary but received the following answer: "We cannot keep that promise, there's a war going on."

The Jewish Agency then contacted Anthony Eden, who was Britain's Foreign Secretary at that time, with a series of requests. The negotiations should be undertaken, a declaration was to be published opening the doors to Jewish refugees and the Swiss government would be requested to give safe conduct papers to all the Jews who requested them. The Hungarian rail workers were to be informed that anyone cooperating in the deportation of the Jews would be considered a war criminal. The railroad tracks used by the death trains to Birkenau and the camp itself were to be bombed. Such a bombing would serve as proof that the Allies were condemning the murder of the Jews.

After months of discussions, delays and consultation with the other allies, Under Secretary of Foreign Affairs Law replied: "The British air force high command must reject the bombing proposal because of the very serious technical problems that are associated with it."

The "supplies for blood" deal was officially rejected by the *Times* and the BBC; the answer effectively cancelled the last desperate proposals of the Jewish Agency. The fate of thousands of Jews was sealed.

To complete picture of the negotiations with Eichmann, Brand's wife also testified, since she remained in Budapest after her husband left and saw Eichmann on about ten occasions. Hansi Brand was one of the few witnesses who answered the question whether she could positively identify the defendant answered without any hesitation: "Certainly, yes."

Mrs. Brand spoke about the negotiations of Dr. Kastner with Eichmann and his staff and the huge sums of money given to the Nazis. She saw with her own eyes the start of the tragic *fussmarch*, the march on foot that Eichmann set up to move thousands of Jews from Budapest to Vienna in the dead of winter. Most of them died along the way.

She was given the difficult task of keeping Eichmann on track even once it became clear that the negotiations had basically failed. She was arrested by the Hungarian police and in spite of the torture she was subjected to, she did not reveal what Eichmann called a "state secret."

The defendant told her during another meeting that her silence had saved her life. But at the same time he told her to cable her husband that "The windmills will begin to turn once again."

Wednesday, May 31

Today the persecutions in Hungary were again being discussed. Joel and Hansi Brand ended their testimony without adding much that was new to the awful story of "supplies for blood." Hansi Brand said that Eichmann never kept any of his promises. He was supposed to suspend the deportations to Auschwitz to allow the negotiations to begin. "But the day after my husband left," she said, "the trains resumed their ride to the gas chambers." To Judge Halevy's question as to whether the Jewish Committee had considered killing Eichmann, the witness answered: "We discussed it among ourselves but we were a rescue committee, not a bunch of heroes. And above all we feared that someone even worse could be sent over instead…"

Joel Brand recalled the relations with the heads of the Committee and the dissent that characterized the various Nazi groups in Budapest. "Becher is free and lives in Germany today. He became very rich thanks to the possessions stolen from the Hungarian Jews." Regarding his meeting with Lord Moyne, Brand said: "I was being held in a sort of prison in Cairo. I was being questioned every day. At times the British officers would take me to a club. One evening I was introduced to a tall thin civilian. It was Lord Moyne. He also asked me whether the Nazis were serious about freeing the Jews. Then he added:

"'One million Jews? What would I do with them? Where would I put them?'"

Lord Moyne was murdered in Cairo a few months later by two Palestinian Jewish terrorists; that night he certainly had no idea that he had signed his own death sentence.

During the afternoon session Moshé Rosenberg took the stand. He was in charge of the rescue operation for the Budapest Jewish community. The main activity was to smuggle young people into Romania or Yugoslavia and have the Jews from the provinces come into Budapest. When they arrived they received false documents, money, and a place to stay. But while many managed to cross the Romanian border, few reached Budapest and the others were deported. Why? The witness tried to give an answer: "My brother remained in the village with his family. I sent him some money and false documents, begging him to come to Budapest. He didn't even answer me and was deported. But perhaps I was being naïve. He should have shaved his beard, changed his clothes, lose his Jewish identity overnight. How could he possibly believe that God would have protected him better that way rather than in his village?"

Perhaps it was because of this psychological attitude that the Nazis were able to take full advantage of that holds the key to their awful success.

Today the prosecution once again offered a series of documents connecting Eichmann to his responsibilities. One of these is a telegram that Veesenmayer, then the German ambassador to Budapest, sent to the Ministry of Foreign Affairs on July 25, 1944. Switzerland was getting ready to welcome 40,000 Hungarian Jews and 1000 children who were later to emigrate to Palestine. The ambassador wrote: "But Eichmann says that Himmler surely doesn't approve the project and he is intent upon changing the Führer's decision. In any case Eichmann proposes to deport those Jews before they can complete the paper-work for their emigration."

Thursday, June 1

The *fussmarsch*, the death march that Eichmann had decided to arrange in order to move some 50,000 Jews from Budapest to Vienna during the winter at the end of 1944, was recounted this morning by Ariva Fleishmann.

The witness told the court how she was captured by the Hungarian Nazis immediately following the fall of the Regent Horthy. Old men, children, pregnant women were assembled in unbelievable conditions in a brick factory. The march began the following day. "We walked four across all day long. At night the column of 1500 to 2000 people had to find shelter in a barn or sleep outside. My mother was in the column behind me. She dragged herself for five days, then was unable to go on. I know that she was shot where she fell just like all those who dropped to the ground along the way. It was in November and there was heavy rain. After one month we reached a camp in Austria. Typhus and dysentery were killing many people. When a woman gave birth the camp commandant arrived saying that he wanted to see how a human being is born. The infant didn't survive more than one hour in those conditions. A train full of wounded people arrived one day. I found an acquaintance who was dying and only asked for some water. I took a canteen and filled it, the commandant saw me and threw the canteen away."

The prosecution then introduced the documents proving how Eichmann had organized the march and kept to his initial orders in spite of the protests of his own staff.

General Hans Jüttner and *Obersturmbannführer* Höss, came to Budapest on November 16. They had seen the results of the death march on the sides of the Vienna-to-Budapest highway and were both outraged. Jüttner insisted that it be interrupted. Eichmann was absent and Wisliceny as his replacement issued the orders. When Eichmann returned he became furious: he demanded that the march resume and threatened to have Wisliceny court-martialed. He was forced to relent, however, when Wisliceny in turn threatened to go to Himmler, since the march clearly contradicted his orders.

Lázló Gordon is the sole survivor of a large family and was deported from Budapest to Poland in 1941 because he was not a Hungarian citizen. Along with other young men he was forced to dig long trenches that he thought were anti-tank ditches. But the following day the executions began and some 300 Jews were killed in each ditch. On the trucks they were using there was a sign that read "German Winter Welfare Assistance." In just a few days some 26,000 people were shot. Scores of corpses were floating downstream in the nearby Dniester River. The witness was able to escape and return to Budapest, but he was arrested once again on April 15, 1944.

"They took me to the Majestic Hotel and questioned me at length. I was facing a wall and they were hitting me repeatedly. When I turned around I saw an SS officer who looked satisfied with the way things were going: it was Eichmann and I can recognize him without any hesitation."

Friday, June 2

In this morning's session, the only one to be held today, two witnesses discussed the execution of Jewish prisoners of war in the Polish army during the winter of 1940.

Avraham Buchman was in the Polish army and was taken prisoner in 1939. The Jews were immediately separated and sent to a special camp, Stalag 32. A few weeks later came the transfer to Lublin. "We were forced to march for days on end in thirty degrees below zero and without any shoes. Along the way the SS were shooting prisoners ten at a time. At Biala Podolska we were divided into two groups. One group of a few hundred prisoners was killed in the forest and we could hear the shooting all day. One of us told the officer in charge that he was protesting since it was against international conventions to kill prisoners of war. The SS officer replied that he had orders from Berlin to eliminate us all but that he had decided to spare one group for the construction of an airport located nearby."

The prosecutor then began a new and final chapter about the extermination camps. This is how he addressed that issue during his initial account.

The Camps

The Nazi concentration camps were meant to reinforce the dictatorship and to terrorize the opposition. There were hundreds of concentration, assembly, and transit camps but where the Jews were concerned they all served one purpose: extermination. Even if the Nazis had not enacted systems for the direct massacre, the prisoners would have died of exhaustion and illness in any case. I shall only discuss the extermination camps that had been set up from the start to apply the so-called "final solution," where millions of Jews were to die.

The idea of killing the Jews with poison gas is already mentioned in Hitler's book, *Mein Kampf.* During World War II, Odilo Globocnik undertook the first experiments and Eichmann adopted the method. He went to Auschwitz to decide with Höss what would be the best location for the gas chambers; then he supplied the "Zykon-B" gas most frequently used and during the final days of the war he even thought of using gas to exterminate the Jews at Theresienstadt.

The camp at Maidanek near Lublin was built in 1941. The gas chambers were working one year later; the Warsaw Jews arrived in 1943 by the tens of thousands. Typhus was rampant and the cure was to be shot to death. Mothers were forcibly separated from their children; at times the children would be butchered in front of them. At Maidanek, the only place where the children were treated with any kindness, at the entrance of the gas chambers there was an SS guard who would give them a piece of candy. Some 200,000 Jews were to die there.

Treblinka is in the province of Warsaw. The camouflage was perfect: a false railroad station bearing the sign of an imaginary restaurant welcomed the prisoners. The sick, the aged, and the children were sent directly to the "hospital" where as soon as they entered the SS would shoot them in the back of the head. All the clothing was to be surrendered on arrival: some two hundred freight cars full were shipped to Germany. Women had all their hair cut before being killed and this was also shipped to Germany. The victims were then herded and squeezed into the gas chambers, a diesel engine would start, and the exhaust fumes would kill everyone inside. As soon as the poison gas was gone gold teeth were pulled from the corpses that were then thrown into the pits. A man was still alive when he was thrown in and managed to escape but the local peasants handed him back to the camp commandant, who beat him to death.

In August 1943 a group of Jews rebelled and was able to escape after setting fire to some of the barracks. A few months later the Germans plowed over the camp and some Ukrainian peasants were brought there to live. 700,000 Jews were killed at Treblinka.

At Chelmno, near Lodz, the victims were immediately killed. On arrival they were told to undress and then they boarded the "death bus": a bus that had been sealed shut so the exhaust fumes would kill 80 to 100 people at a time. Some 350,000 Jews were put to death there.

From that camp as well all clothing was shipped to the "Winter Assistance Campaign" in Germany that complained once that it had received a jacket that still had the yellow star.

Sobibor, where some 250,000 Jews died, was located near Lublin. Not too far away on the road from Lublin and Lwow there was the Belzec camp. An eyewitness described the scene as follows: "The sealed doors of the freight train were opened and the people were ordered to come out. Each one must hand over his or her clothing, including all eyeglasses. Women go to a barber who quickly cuts their hair off and collects it in potato sacks. Then the march begins. Men, women, and children completely naked are made to march together. One of the SS guards smiles and says: "You will not be harmed in any way. Just breathe in deeply; the inhaling disinfects." A ray of hope encourages everyone to walk into the gas chambers without any resistance. They go up a few steps and then understand what is about to happen. Mothers hold their naked children against their chest. They hesitate but move along in silence pushed by those coming in behind them and by the whips of the SS. Many are praying. Then the doors close while the others remain outside in the dead of winter. But then the diesel engine fails to work. A professor of hygiene at Marburg University tells me: "They are whispering as if they were in a synagogue." Finally the engine starts and within 32 minutes everyone is dead. Families remain together even in death holding hands. Then the Jewish workers open up the doors and drag out the corpses soiled with urine and sweat. Some of them open the mouths of the dead to pull out gold teeth using a pair of pliers. "Others are looking for diamonds and gold…" The Nazis killed 600,000 Jews at Belzec.

But the death factory for millions was Auschwitz, which shall remain as a symbol of horror and infamy in human history. Auschwitz is the German name of a small town near Krakow. According to the camp commandant, Höss, about two and a half million people were killed there and another half million died of disease, hunger, and torture. There were also thousands of gypsies, Soviet prisoners of war, and political opponents. But the Jews arrived by the millions.

The camp was surrounded by a high voltage electric fence. With a move of his finger Dr. Josef Mengele would select people for the work teams. In the camp's archives the cards indicate that they had been sent there by the IV B4 Section. Eichmann visited the camp, issued instructions for the selections and the bounty that reached extraordinary proportions was so great as to have an impact on the diamond market in Switzerland.

The killing was done in many different ways but mostly using the gas chambers where 2000 people would be assembled at a time. The "shower" they were promised was actually a gas that turned the two thousand people inside into corpses in twenty-five minutes and were then sent to the crematoriums. Later on the victims were thrown into the Vistula River.

Medical experiments were also taking place at Auschwitz on prisoners used as human guinea pigs. Women were sterilized, men castrated, and fuel or paraffin was injected into their veins.

The Germans tried to cover up all traces of these murders and in 1942 Eichmann gave orders to burn the corpses that were previously buried in the pits. Later on, the ovens of the crematoriums and the gas chambers were also blown up. The Nazis believed that their crimes would not be discovered. But their secret had been revealed; we must now act according to the warning given by an unknown poet who died at Auschwitz: *Our army will advance, skulls and jaws / one bone next to the other in a pitiless line / We, the persecuted will scream against you / Those who were murdered are asking for justice from your hands.*

Israel Gutman testified today about Maidanek. He took part in the Warsaw ghetto revolt in 1943 but was forced out of his bunker by the mustard gas the Nazis were using. "We reached the camp at Maidanek and were subjected to a first selection: one group was immediately sent to the gas chambers. We were about 800 to each hut, on three levels. The work was to run while we dragged some stones, and crushed them to build a road. I caught pneumonia and was admitted to the hospital: I was the first one to enjoy that kind of treatment because—until then sick Jews were summarily shot. From the hospital's windows I saw a group of naked men on their way to the gas chambers. There was a ten-year-old child who was holding a younger child in his arms. Two SS guards were laughing as they looked on.

"We also had to defend ourselves from the Kapos inside the camp. Most of them were common criminals who enjoyed better conditions and they would beat us with a heavy iron bar they were equipped with. After several attempts I managed to join a group that was being transferred to Auschwitz. There I immediately found the camp's secret organization. We tried to help with a piece of bread, with medicine, but we also tried to take violent action.

"A few women managed to bring some explosives out of the factory they were working in and passed them on to a *Sonderkommando*, one of the teams handling the crematoriums, that in turn were periodically killed. Once they understood that their situation was hopeless, they revolted. It was November 6, 1944, and the ovens were operating relentlessly for the Hungarian Jews. They blew up a crematorium and killed a few SS guards, then escaped. But they were caught and executed."

The prosecution introduced a few documents regarding the Mufti of Jerusalem, Haj Amin el-Husseini. In a letter dated May 13, 1943, to Foreign Minister von Ribbentrop, the Mufti requested that the emigration of 5,000 Jewish children from Bulgaria, Romania, and Hungary be prevented. Similar letters were also sent to the governments of the countries involved. To the Romanian foreign minister the Mufti wrote: "The Jews should be sent to a country like Poland, where they can do no harm."

The letters were mailed from Rome since the Mufti was a guest of the Fascist government at the time. He also sent a draft of a declaration to be issued by Italy and Germany stating that the Jewish National Home in Palestine was illegal and that the Jewish problem in Palestine should be solved in the same manner as the Axis countries had already done. A few weeks ago, Lord Russell described this project as "a Balfour Declaration in reverse."

Monday, June 3

We were convinced that we had heard every possible form of human cruelty in the course of this trial. But the chapter that began yesterday about the death camps goes beyond every other atrocity. Six witnesses told the court today about their incredible suffering at the camps of Maidanek, Sobibor, and Chelmno. The three camps had a life of their own, with a different organization, but the same overall objective: the systematic massacre of thousands of innocent people.

Dov Freiberg was fifteen when he was deported to Sobibor in 1942. "Each train," he said, "would follow the same procedure: the people would get off quickly; men and women were separated and sent to the showers. In the courtyard an SS guard gave the same speech: 'You are being sent to the Ukraine to work in the fields. But there is very little time. Give your valuables at the window and enter the showers immediately.' The men would undress and the doors would open: these were the gas chambers. An orchestra was playing music nearby without stopping. When there was some time the Nazis would engage in every form of torture: they would kill with their whips, encourage the guard dogs to bite, and beat people to a pulp. They would always invent something new: one of the prisoners was forced to run on all fours barking like a dog for a few days. They wanted to turn us into animals. A few attempts to escape failed. A Dutch Jewish captain tried to organize a revolt. When he was captured he refused to give the names of his comrades, so as a reprisal seventy members of his group were decapitated in front of him. A revolt took place anyway and 300 prisoners were able to escape.

"On one occasion, and only one, did an SS guard have a more humane attitude, but a few days later he requested a transfer. I was assigned to various tasks. One day they told us to undress and then carry off the naked bodies of a few prisoners. It was an awful feeling. While one of them was on my very shoulder, he asked in a whisper: "Is it far away?""

Michael Podchlebnik is one of the four survivors of the camp at Chelmno. The procedure was different there: instead of gas chambers they used the so-called "death bus." The prisoners were made to enter a bus that was tightly sealed. The engine would start and screaming could be heard as the bus ran for a short time. Then a few minutes later it would stop on the side of a large pit. "Every day they took us into the forest to dig these huge pits. When the bus arrived we had to wait two or three minutes for the gas fumes to lift completely. Then we would pull out the corpses and place them in the pit. When I was handling the third one I suddenly recognized my wife and two boys. I threw myself on the ground next to them because I wanted to die. But an SS guard dragged me away. That night I tried to commit suicide in the camp but my comrades stopped me: 'As long as your eyes are open you must hope,' they told me. A few days later I managed to escape as they were taking us to work."

Crematoriums, gas chambers, death buses: all the instruments of modern technology were being used for the massacres.

Mordechai Zuravsky was at Chelmno a few years later in 1944. Often the driver of the terrible bus would end up among his passengers with a bullet in the back of the neck as they were being pulled out dead or near death. A witness recalled an inspection at Maidanek by Eichmann and Servatius broke his usual silence to cross-examine him. Another saw Eichmann twice at Sobibor, in 1942 and 1943.

Tuesday, June 6

Today six more witnesses recalled the killings in the Nazi concentration camps. They were assigned to extract gold teeth, cut off hair, collect clothing; every item was to be saved, carefully inventoried, and used in the rear of the front lines. Everything was done scientifically, according to industrial methods.

Simon Srebnik recalled: "One Saturday I was walking with my father in the Lodz ghetto; I heard a shot and my father fell to the ground next to me, dead. I was thirteen at the time. I was loaded on a truck and deported to Chelmno camp. My feet were in chains for two years from 1943 to 1945. I had to jump if I wanted to move. My job was to extract gold teeth from the corpses and take care of the personal belongings. Once, in a bunch of papers, I came across a picture of my mother. Two days before liberation the Nazis took us to the forest in groups of five to shoot us. I was hit but remained alive, motionless among the corpses and managed to save my life."

Kalman Teigmann gave a description of Treblinka. As he was speaking there were pictures behind him of a model of the camp created by a carpenter who had built the original barracks. To give the camp a less threatening appearance, a false railroad station had also been built with train schedules, flowers and a large clock. It was on an unused portion of tracks. The charade, however, had to be kept up for as long as possible: each deportee was given a bar of soap and a towel and sent to the showers that were really the gas chambers. A big diesel engine would start up and after some 40 to 45 minutes the doors were opened wide and the corpses came tumbling down on the slightly inclined floor to be burned. At times when the doors opened the children were still alive because they had curled up on the floor and they were then finished off by the SS guards. Following Himmler's visit in 1943 they began digging up the bodies, originally buried in the common pits, in order to burn them: the Nazis wanted to leave no traces behind. "Finally, with the help of the oldest prisoners, we organized a revolt. A detainee in charge of disinfection sprayed the barracks with gasoline; then we set them on fire and escaped."

The prosecution introduced, among many documents, a long report by Dr. Gerstein on the death camps. It is a terrifying account, even more so because it is the work of an exceptional witness. Even though he was a member of the SS, he was an anti-Nazi in charge of supplying the camps with Zyklon-B gas. Starting in 1942 he told everything he knew to the Swedish ambassador in Berlin, hoping that this would interrupt the killings. He also kept all the invoices for gas supplies that were given to the court today. There was enough to kill eight million people.

Wednesday, June 7

"I see them...they are looking at me..." Stuttering these words, today's first witness lost consciousness and was taken to the hospital.

Just before that, when the prosecutor asked why he was hiding behind the pseudonym of "Kazetnik 135633" that he used to publish several books, Yehiel Dinur answered: "This is not a pseudonym. I was writing the history of another planet: Auschwitz. The inhabitants of that planet had no names, only a number: Kazetnik internee number so-and-so. If I am alive today I owe it to the oath I took to them to recount everything. That gave me the strength to survive for two years.

I shall keep this name until humanity understands that the crucifixion of an entire people took place. They are looking at me. I see them lining up. I see them…"

Today's witnesses described the Auschwitz death camp, the largest and most organized of the Nazi "lagers." Two witnesses testified behind closed doors during the only such private session until now. They were sterilized at Auschwitz and today they have families in Israel, having adopted children. That is the reason to protect their identity.

Josef Kleinmann, a Jerusalem carpenter, was deported to Auschwitz at age 14. "We were separated from our families right away. One day the barracks commander began whipping a boy. We counted the blows…twenty, thirty…but the boy didn't utter a sound, not a scream or a tear. The blows reached fifty and finally were over. The boy then told us: 'It was worth it. I had brought a prayer book to my fellow prisoners.'"

Dr. Josef Mengele, the terror inside the camp, was in charge of the selections. One day he called 200 boys outside and had a plank nailed to a specific height: those who came in lower had to be eliminated. "I tried to fill my shoes with rocks so that my head would touch the plank. But I could see that would not be enough. So I managed to slip into the group destined to remain alive. The others were herded into a truck and began to scream. I never heard such screams before. They were certainly not the first victims to go to the gas chambers at Auschwitz, but contrary to the others they already knew what was in store for them."

Aharon Beilin is a doctor who was in charge of handling the gypsies. "Eighteen thousand arrived and were infected with unusual illnesses. Mengele gave orders to undertake scientific research on them. Then they were all sent to the gas chambers. Some gypsies were wearing German army uniforms. Others didn't want to be examined by Jewish doctors. But all of them met the same fate.

"The Nazis picked the Jewish holidays to eliminate the sick and the weak. Zyklon-B gas was used in the camp as a disinfectant and to hunt down rats. We knew, however, that the same gas was being used to kill the inmates. Every three months all the Jews of the *Sonderkommando*, the men working inside the crematoriums and the gas chambers, were completely replaced. To enter that group meant having three months to live. I was able to hide and save my life. In January 1945 the dreadful march on foot began. Those unable to walk were killed in the snow. Of 25,000 men who left Auschwitz, only 60 survived. Three days before liberation I was reduced to a "musselman," as they named those about to die of hunger.

"Mengele saw me and recognized who I was. I understood that he wished to eliminate a dangerous witness to his pseudoscientific experiments. Then I lost consciousness and woke up in a hospital after the liberation."

Yehuda Bacon saw his family being taken to the gas chambers. The group of boys he was with brought wood to the crematoriums and then scattered the ashes of the dead on the roads to prevent vehicles from slipping. During the winter the boys kept warm inside the gas chambers. The witness is a painter and the court examined some of the paintings of camp scenes he had made.

Thursday, June 8

Five of the six witnesses heard today have a small black number tattooed inside their left arm: they are Auschwitz survivors. Vera Alexander arrived in 1942 and became a block leader. "It wasn't easy to follow orders and help the inmates at the same time. But I did what I could. I got sick and was discharged from the infirmary before I could recover. I wanted to go back. At night I managed to sneak into the cellar. A few women were sitting near the wall and I recognized some who were from my town. I went in closer to speak to them but they were all motionless…dead. I ran away. In one of the children's barracks I saw one of Dr. Mengele's experiments. He took two gypsy twins and two other twins and tied the veins in their arms together. A few days later the sutures were infected: the experiment was over. A Hungarian mother managed to bring her daughter into our barracks. This was forbidden. The girl was taken and thrown into a crematorium. That evening the mother threw herself on the high voltage electric fence."

Nahum Hoch is one of three or four persons in the world to emerge from a gas chamber alive. "I was among the last thousand boys at Auschwitz. They placed us in rows of five. We didn't want to walk and knew where they were taking us. To make us move they fired shots at our legs and forced us to go. We entered a large room resembling a public bath. They told us to undress and hang our clothes on numbered hooks to retrieve them later. But we knew they were lying. One of us yelled out: "Let's sing, boys!" Then a large door opened and we went into a dark room. Some were crying, others recited the prayer Shema' Israel, 'Listen, Israel.' I remained motionless, frozen. Suddenly the doors opened again and I was sent off with 50 of the strongest to unload a train of potatoes. The others went back to the gas chambers and the doors closed on them forever."

Ghedalia Ben Zvi, an art teacher, worked for one year in the so-called "Canada" sector. "We had to unload the suitcases from the trains, sort out the perishables, send clothing to the workshops where they would take off the yellow star and unthread the pockets to find any hidden objects. Every week we would load twenty railroad cars filled with clothing to Germany. Then after about one year I was sent to clean the inmate's trains. On the floor were the bodies of those who had died of suffocation; they were tangled up in a knot that was very hard to unravel. Under that heap a 10-year-old girl was still alive. She walked a few steps then an SS guard went up to her and shot her in the head."

The words of the witnesses, interrupted by sobbing, were illustrated with a few documentary films shown in court. Nazi attempts to cover up traces of the killings were useless. Thousands of bodies in huge stacks with their eyes open and their gaping mouths distorted in a scream that perhaps no one even heard, the mountains of eyeglasses, the human hair, the dolls—all serve as proof of a well-organized massacre that the world can barely believe ever took place.

One of the judges was crying. Many journalists, the only ones allowed to view the film for security reasons, were also emotional. In the shadows of the courtroom Eichmann sat with his impassive mask, writing long notes to his defense lawyer.

From the left: Foreign Minister J. von Ribbentrop, Adolf Hitler and Italian Foreign Minister Galeazzo Ciano, August 13, 1939.

Reinhard Heydrich, Head of the RSHA and Himmler's
deputy until his assassination in Prague in 1942.

Heinrich Himmler, Reichsführer SS
and Head of the German Police.

Adolf Eichmann, Head of RSHA *Amt* IV
B 4 in charge of Jewish Affairs.

Heinrich Müller, Head of the Gestapo
and Eichmann's direct superior.

Walter Schellenberg, Head of RSHA *Amt* VI Foreign Espionage and later Head of all German intelligence.

Wilhelm Höttl, RSHA foreign intelligence agent
and a friend of Eichmann's.

Odilo Globocnik, former Gauleiter of Vienna
and death camp organizer.

Yad Vashem

Beit Haam, the People's House in Jerusalem where the trial was held in 1961.

GPO State of Israel

The author (far left with glasses) in the newsroom during the trial.

Judges: Moshe Landau, presiding *(center)*, Benjamin Halevy *(left)*
and Yitzhak Raveh *(right)*.

Yad Vashem

Defense attorney Robert Servatius addresses the court
as Prosecutor Hausner sits on his right.

Yad Vashem

Yad Vashem

Prosecutor Gideon Hausner

GPO State of Israel

Assistant Prosecutor Gabriel Bach (standing) with Gideon Hausner
and Defense Attorney Robert Servatius.

Abba Kovner.

GPO State of Israel

GPO State of Israel

Yehiel Dinur Katzetnik.

GPO State of Israel

Hulda Campagnano.

GPO State of Israel

Zivia Lubetkin Zuckermann with Prosecutor Hausner.

GPO State of Israel

Yitzhak Zuckermann.

Joel Brand testifying at the Eichmann trial in Jerusalem in 1961.

Friday, June 9

The most serious accusations against Eichmann seem to originate with his comrades-in-arms from the netherworld. Following the deposition of Wisliceny, the prosecutor introduced the testimony of Auschwitz commandant Rudolf Höss today. During his testimony to the Polish court that would sentence him to death, he had also stated, among other things, that: "Himmler summoned me in 1941. He informed me that Hitler had ordered the start of the 'Final Solution.' I was to contact Eichmann to get the details. I was given broad orders: all the Jews shipped in by Eichmann were to be immediately exterminated without wasting one hour. The camp's installations allowed at the most to gas and burn 10,000 persons per day. When the first trains came in from Hungary, Eichmann accompanied them personally to try and step up the pace of the operation. He also set the dates when they were to go to the gas chambers. Just before liberation, Eichmann told me that according to his calculations there were 2.5 million Jews that had been eliminated at Auschwitz. It was Europe's largest camp. The crematoria were working day and night."

The presentation of witnesses and of documents by the prosecution had to end for today but will be extended into next week. The defense has raised an objection regarding the accuracy of the Eichmann memoirs dictated to the Nazi journalist Willem Sassen some years ago, that have since been published by an American weekly (*Life* magazine). Sassen is said to have made changes that were not authorized and should therefore be called to testify. The court will decide the issue on Monday.

In the course of the hearing the prosecutor recalled that Eichmann was providing the Nazi racial study institutes with skulls and human skeletons.

Monday, June 12

The prosecution completed its work today, thereby bringing the first phase of the Eichmann trial to an end. Over one hundred witnesses testified in the course of 74 hearings, each one with his or her own personal odyssey, and 1,400 documents have been introduced as evidence. It will be up to the judges to determine whether or not the defendant is guilty. What is clear is that for the first time public opinion has been offered a complete documentation on the massacre of the Jewish people.

The defense has won the procedural battle regarding the memoirs dictated by Eichmann to Sassen, at least in part: the court agreed to enter only a small segment of the memoirs with the handwritten corrections made by the defendant. The defense objected that the document was incomplete and had been written while under the influence of alcohol and therefore it was not admissible.

The prosecution called its two final witnesses today. The first spoke of Jewish partisans fighting in the forests of Bielorussia; the second recalled the moving encounter of the soldiers of the Jewish Brigade with the living skeletons that had survived the extermination camps.

The attorney Hoter-Ishai said: "I went looking for survivors throughout Europe and found people that resembled decapitated or amputated corpses. Half of the survivors, some 50,000 in total, died after the liberation: they no longer had enough strength to live. When they would see us they would kiss the Star of David that was painted on our trucks—the same star they had to carry as an infamous badge—or they tried to touch the emblem sewn on our sleeves. Today it seems almost like a miracle: but that encounter gave them a new reason to live. They knew that the Jews of Palestine were waiting for them."

In order to give the defense enough time to consult the documents that had been introduced, the court suspended its hearings for one week. Only then will we know whether the defense will call Eichmann to testify thereby exposing the defendant to the risks of cross-examination.

Tuesday, June 20

Eichmann has spoken at last—not in monosyllables as he did at the start of the trial, but at length as the first defense witness. To the three possibilities offered to him by the presiding judge—to give a statement, to remain silent, or to testify under oath—he preferred the last option. However, he refused to swear on the Gospel and instead used the formula "I swear in the name of God."

Defense attorney Servatius said in his opening statement: "Two worlds are facing one another in this trial: the victims and the dictatorship. The defendant was under the obligation to carry out the orders of the political authorities and it is pure fantasy to allege that he was worse than Hitler. Eichmann is not responsible for the extermination of the Jews; he did not issue the orders for those massacres and even less did he carry them out. He actually attempted to put an end to them through the proposal to have one million Jews emigrate. The defendant was carrying out orders, he was not issuing them. Those who were truly guilty were therefore holding the levers in the highest positions in the state."

From his glass booth in his monotone and metallic-sounding voice, while being respectful of the judges who allowed him to remain seated, Eichmann began to respond to his defense attorney's questions.

He began by saying that the statement that he wanted to come to Israel to stand trial was extorted from him in Buenos Aires while he was tied to a bed.

Then while reminiscing about the beginnings of his career he went on: "My superiors had given me orders to encourage Jewish emigration. The Zionists wanted emigration to Palestine and I helped them. The thought of a Jewish State came to me like the egg of Christopher Columbus. I proposed Madagascar as a possible solution or any other country that would put the Jews on solid ground.

"In 1939 Himmler was appointed Reich Commissioner for the integrity of the German people. His orders were creating complete chaos, especially in the realm of transportation. Every Gauleiter [regional Nazi leader] was acting independently and the trains would remain idle for days on end. Then Heydrich gave me a special department to coordinate the various activities and in particular the train schedules.

"Starting in 1940 I was responsible for Jewish affairs under Müller, the head of Section IV of the Reich Main Security Office [RSHA]. However, I had no kind of autonomy whatsoever. Had I allowed anyone to emigrate contrary to Himmler's orders, Müller would have found out and would have asked me for an explanation. None of us had any special position and we were all under Müller's scrutiny."

There was murmuring among the audience when it heard those words that seemed to fit a minor railroad official. The presiding judge demanded that there be silence in the courtroom.

The prosecutor at the beginning of the hearing introduced a few documents to complete the material being presented.

Among other documents he offered a report by Herbert Kappler (the local SS commander) on the arrest of 1,200 Jews in Rome on October 16, 1943.

Wednesday, June 21

Eichmann continued his testimony today on his favorite subject: the internal organization of the Gestapo and the duties of the various sections. His bureaucratic language is so prolix, abstruse, and technical, that the presiding judge and the defense attorney had to ask him to use short and clear sentences.

Acronyms, Roman and Arabic numerals, three color schemes follow one another in an almost incomprehensible jumble; the only one who can understand it is the defendant, who is perfectly comfortable in the academic chair on Nazi administration that he appears to be occupying.

Eichmann gave a long list of offices that were more important than his with respect to the Jews, each one with its set of letters: III B Race and Public Health was in charge of mixed marriages; III B4 Emigration and Transfers of Population; VII BI Scientific Research on Jews and Freemasons. That last section was in charge of determining what a Sephardic or Iranian Jew was but at times it simply noted the appropriate page in the Jewish Encyclopedia.

Then Eichmann quickly accused Globke, saying that Division I at the Ministry of the Interior, which he was responsible for, took the initiative of revoking the German citizenship of the Jews to allow for the confiscation of their possessions.

"The deportations were organized by the central offices for population transfers, together with local officials, the gendarmerie, and the police. My department was to provide the convoys and establish schedules to ensure efficiency and speed, which actually also benefited the inmates themselves."

Finally, the few survivors of the deportations know who to thank for the comfortable trip they had to take.

To prove how little freedom Eichmann enjoyed, Servatius tells us that he did not even possess an autonomous telephone switchboard.

"In Hungary I wouldn't have been able to take any decisions that went against the local SS commander," Eichmann adds, just to be sure: "I personally had no special position with my commander, Müller; and actually according to the documents shown here Müller was issuing orders directly to my subordinate, Günther, without my knowledge. I could make concrete proposals, but final decisions belonged to my chief, Müller, and to Foreign Minister von Ribbentrop who also supervised the Jewish issues experts abroad. I recall among these Wisliceny in Slovakia, and Richter in Romania. All their reports had to go through the head of the diplomatic mission."

To a question from Judge Halevy, Eichmann answers by giving an explanation of Ernst Kaltenbrunner's position in 1941. "At that time he was the head of the RSHA intelligence services that he had set up with Schellenberg as a counterweight to Canaris and his organization."

It appears that Eichmann has memorized the answers he intends to give even before the questions are asked by his defense lawyer and his line of defense is rather simple: Department IV, of which he was part, was not the only one to handle Jewish matters, since many other sections were also involved and, with regard to the section he was responsible for, Müller was clearly in charge.

It would appear to be a rather naïve position to take; the principle of direct responsibility had already been established at Nuremberg and the convenient screen of orders issued from above didn't provide any excuse.

Today we understood the care and urgency with which Eichmann was following the introduction of documents by the prosecution: the whole defense tactic seems to be centered on archival detail. Servatius admitted that the defendant, with his observations, reminds him of things that he, Servatius, has forgotten. Clearly within the Nazi alchemy Eichmann is the only one who knows his way around and he relishes every minute detail, as he takes up to ten minutes to answer the chief justice when he was asked the exact day in 1939 when he was summoned to Berlin.

In the course of the first two days of his testimony Eichmann described himself as a minor employee whose only task was to coordinate transportation, set up train schedules, and avoid having idle railroad cars on some non-operating tracks. In other words, Eichmann was just an all-purpose railroad engineer. Using this excuse he intends to slip away like an eel through the net set up by the prosecution; the famous *juden referenten,* Wisliceny and Richter among them, were in the end submitted to the approval of the Ministry of Foreign Affairs and carrying out its orders; the deportations were ordered by Himmler and Heydrich; if a fast pace led to a few deaths it was clearly the responsibility of local authorities. And so on.

Thursday, June 22

In his nasty and picayune way that can become a ghoulish kind of black comedy, Eichmann continued today to throw every responsibility back to his superiors. "They ordered me to go to the east only when there were problems in scheduling the trains. I was neither the moving force nor the initiator of the evacuations. Müller would not tolerate any personal initiatives on our part. My department would only transmit the evacuation orders it received from Müller, Heydrich, and at times from Himmler himself. It is only natural that once they reached the lower levels of the hierarchy the orders would become more detailed."

In Eichmann's vocabulary deportations became evacuations, but the death camps could have no euphemisms and he never mentioned them.

This approach that was used yesterday already shows some cracks in it today. To the chief judge's question regarding the reason Eichmann approved a memo of a meeting about the deportation of the Poles, the defendant muttered: "I can't remember…maybe it was to do things in orderly fashion…perhaps communications in the area were not satisfactory…"

But then vanity and conceit had the upper hand and for the first time Eichmann admitted that he had created something on his own: the Madagascar project, the island where the European Jews were to be concentrated: "My efforts tended to provide the Jews with firm ground to stand on…"

Then in a long disquisition, Eichmann explained why the special "W" fund was set up. "To simplify matters and avoid having to contact the Ministry of Finance each time a Jew would remit into this fund an amount that was meant to cover the expenses relating to his evacuation."

Eichmann had therefore invented the device of having the victims pay for their own deportation!

"On the other hand the Jews had lost every right to property since a decree from Division I of the Ministry of the Interior under Hans Globke had made them stateless and allowed the confiscation of their property. Actually, this provided the legal basis that made the deportations possible."

Again today Eichmann is quoting Globke; perhaps this is a small personal vendetta that still leaves us wondering.

Eichmann finally explains the true reason behind the deportations of the Jews: "The rhythm was stepped up after Stalingrad. I think they wanted to divert attention from what was going on at the front and the Reich Minister of Propaganda was looking for a scapegoat."

This was a long suspected reason but still, it did make a considerable impression coming from Eichmann himself.

Friday, June 23

From one day to the next Eichmann is filling in his self portrait: as a small time, second rate officer who drafted a few letters and who signed a few others, but always following orders from his superiors. So the struggle around the rubber stamps, the documents, and letterheads goes on.

On a deportation order of 1942, Heydrich wrote: "For all further details contact the expert Eichmann." The defendant was ready to respond: "I am being mentioned as the expert of Jewish questions at the Main Security Office! But my duties were limited only to Department IV! There is therefore a mistake!"

Eichmann found many mistakes and inaccuracies in the documents that Servatius handed him; as for example on the plan to use gas, that had his initialed approval. "My name was surely used by mistake," the defendant quickly noted.

Eichmann also shed light on the higher echelons of the Reich: they were all lusting for power and jealous of their own prerogatives.

Heydrich called the Wannsee Conference to broaden his responsibilities at the expense of the other ministries; Himmler, the head of the SS, couldn't stand the authority of the Ministry of the Interior and appointed SS officers as the main department heads, placing them under his command.

His wordy explanations went on to such an extent that even the chief judge lost patience and called the defendant to order; he told him clearly, in German: "Give precise answers. We are not in the preliminary investigation and you cannot speak endlessly." Eichmann obsequiously promised to be brief.

But today's revelation, according to Eichmann, is that he was actually a savior of the Jews. "In 1941 a concentration camp commandant was complaining about me because I suddenly forced him to take 20,000 Jews. At a previous inspection tour in the east I saw with my own eyes the preparations for the extermination of the Jews. It was the only time I had the opportunity to make a choice. I preferred sending those 20,000 thousand Jews into that camp, where killings were not yet taking place." Then he added: "When the second wave of deportations began, my job was to coordinate the train schedules with the Ministry of Transportation. I had no idea that the Jews deported to Riga and Minsk were to be exterminated. No one had told us. In 1941 I didn't even know what the expression 'final solution' meant."

"But how can this be," asked Judge Halevy. "Didn't you just say that you witnessed preparations for the extermination and had saved some Jews from being massacred?" As usual, even when faced with a clear contradiction, Eichmann offers a long, detailed reply.

Monday, June 26

Unable to ask for forgiveness or to cry out his hatred, Eichmann keeps on hiding behind a maze of letters and papers. This morning he once again mentioned the sadly famous Wannsee Conference of January 1942, when the extermination of the Jews, the so-called "final solution" was decided.

"Everyone appeared to be eager to collaborate in this final solution, for which even those who hesitated showed unexpected enthusiasm and even pleasure. Heydrich was very pleased with the way the conference was going. I was also satisfied since my position had been confirmed by the facts themselves. In spite of my rather low rank I had attempted to find a more moderate solution by trying to bring a semblance of order within the emigration chaos and setting up the plans for Madagascar. The most important officials of the Reich had taken part in the Wannsee Conference and all I had to do was to obey their orders. After the conference my habit of not making any decision without orders from my superiors became an obsession. I therefore felt like Pontius Pilate: the guilt could not fall upon me." Eichmann then denied having any responsibility for sterilization plans using X-Rays and poisonous plants and for collecting skulls and skeletons of Judeo-Bolsheviks requested and secured by the University of Strasbourg. "As far as sterilization went, my deputy Günther was given secret orders directly from Müller. The skeleton collection of Strasbourg University, in spite of the fact that the letters were addressed to me, were not something I was involved with; these were matters that went beyond my tasks. I never handled sterilization nor the inmates of concentration camps and their transfer. This is clear from the documents I have here."

He is using such complicated language that even his defense attorney must request that he speak clearly.

Eichmann then explains that the Jews were to pay for the transportation costs of their own deportation with special "gifts," but if they were loaded one thousand at a time when there was a maximum load of 700, this was because 700 German soldiers and their gear took up more space than 1000 Jews.

The statement sent waves among the audience and the presiding judge had to recall the orders for silence in the court rather energetically: "You may think you want but do not express your feelings." He said.

The directives for the technical implementation of the deportations and how the secret of their destination was kept, the food and supplies for the convoys, were all signed by Eichmann. This, naturally, was based upon "directives from his superiors that were imposed upon [him] from higher up."

Eichmann then admits to having signed firing squad orders concerning the Jews, but on the basis of orders from SS Chief Himmler transmitted to Gestapo and SD head Müller and from the chief of Section IV to the defendant to be distributed to local police sections.

In 1942 Heydrich was assassinated in Prague and as part of the reprisals 99 children from the Czechoslovakia village of Lidice were deported. Krumey, who received them in Poland, asked Eichmann for instructions, thinking that the children were to be subjected to "special treatment." Eichmann today denies that he had anything to do with the matter. "If Günther answered he did so under direct orders from Müller. I"—and here the pride of little bureaucrat surfaces once more—"would not have waited twenty-four hours to answer a telegram."

Eichmann has obviously forgotten that during the pre-trial examination he already has admitted his responsibility for the fate of the children of Lidice.

Wednesday, June 27

An increasingly bored audience is having difficulty following Adolf Eichmann's mental gyrations as he attempts to explain the twists of the Nazi bureaucratic jungle.

The children of Lidice came up once more this morning. Yesterday Eichmann had claimed that he knew nothing about it; however his defense attorney placed the children's death in doubt when he introduced the vague deposition of a woman claiming that she saw them in Poznan in January 1945. The prosecution replied by introducing the first and last names and ages of the 82 children who ended up in the gas chambers at Chelmno; only ten who were found to be adequate for Germanization were alive at Poznan.

Servatius then presented to the judges an umpteenth Nazi hierarchy chart in three colors drawn by Eichmann, but he notes: "The dotted line that connects the SS command in red to the SD command in blue should actually be a solid line with an arrow." The chief justice quickly observed: "To me it looks like a snake biting its tail… The files that come out of IV B4 return back to it…"

The defense lawyer keeps on sending stacks of documents to the defendant. Eichmann had been personally approached regarding the requisition of a Jewish hospital. The deportation of Polish workers in Germany in 1942 had been ordered by Günther, who was directly under Eichmann's orders. But the unflappable Eichmann repeats the same answers all over again: "My job was only to organize the transportation or at the most some other formality that Müller ordered." In all those years, did Eichmann ever inquire about the destination of those trains that he was able to schedule so efficiently? It doesn't seem to be the case. How many euphemisms in his speech are used to describe brutal massacres and deportations: he mentions "evacuations," "reducing the population at Theresienstadt," "final solution," "special treatment."

The German poet Johan Klepper, who had married a Jewish woman, contacted Eichmann to prevent his wife's deportation. The day after that meeting, distraught at the answer he was given, the poet committed suicide. Eichmann's comment is extremely predictable: "Even in that case I could not act on my own initiative."

To the end Eichmann is attempting to play the card that he was following orders from his superiors. When the chief justice calls him to order asking him to be brief, Eichmann tenses up and responds *Jawohl.* That too is an order.

Wednesday, June 28

This morning attorney Servatius returned to the case of Mrs. Cozzi, which had prompted the intercession of the Italian Ministry of Foreign Affairs and even of the Fascist party, without any results. Responding to his defense attorney, Eichmann said: "As it is clear from document T/348, first paragraph, the Jewish woman Cozzi was interned at the Riga ghetto. We had to reject the request for her freedom since Himmler himself had forbidden the freeing of any Jew who had been placed in a ghetto. I could certainly not ask the head of the SS to make an exception. Therefore, the steps that were taken produced no results and in September 1943 Müller, taking advantage of the political changes that had taken place in Italy, closed the file."

Judge Raveh then exclaimed: "But how can this be? We have an order here to deport Cozzi to a concentration camp and it is signed by you!" "It is clear, judge, that I was signing *Im auftrage* or 'in the name of' the commandant. I therefore was only transmitting an order..." Eichmann replies as unflappable as ever.

Servatius, following the order of the prosecution's case, then reaches the Austrian chapter. Eichmann was in Vienna in 1938 to set up the central emigration offices and wrote in a letter at the time that he was hoping for a promotion if the central office was successful. Once more we discover that career advancement was Eichmann's main motivation during those years. In fact, he managed to become "a valued expert," in the words of his supervisor Mr. Six. An expert in the "final solution" naturally. The justification he offers today is mean-minded and picayune: "I wanted the promotion for the organization chart; the rank and pay of a department head were obviously higher than those of a simple section director."

Servatius went on: "What did the witness do when he was told about the famous 'night of broken glass' on November 10, 1938, when the synagogue and its buildings were burned?" "I had finally managed to organize the Jewish groups with a lot of toil and pleasure and now all my work had been destroyed. My first thought was therefore to save the files and the documents held in the burned buildings." We finally learned today what Eichmann's favorite task was: to re-organize the Jewish communities.

"Sometimes I arrived too late. That was the reason why they sent me the telegram cited by the prosecution saying that I was to handle the archives personally. But I had no executive power and could certainly not order any arrests or confiscations. Actually to facilitate emigration I had obtained from the National Bank that the community could keep the amount of $100,000 received from abroad and I also prevented the arrest of the officials at the local Palestine Office. I had also demonstrated the greatest generosity in handing out emigration permits. Dr. Lowenheiz would often come to see me; I had him freed from jail so that he could come back and lead the Vienna community. He always found in me someone who was ready to listen to him. He asked me for the authorization to transfer the remains of Theodore Herzl to Palestine. At that time in Vienna, in March 1939, he would have been unable to discuss such a problem. However, Lowenheiz knew my position on the Jewish problem which, I had understood so well by reading Boehm's book. I was not the right contact to move the remains but I answered by promising my help in exchange for 8,000 additional certificates allowing as many Jews to emigrate to Palestine."

One must acknowledge that it took Eichmann little effort to become an expert in Jewish affairs: he only had to read a single book and take a few Hebrew lessons! But I must regretfully agree with one of the defendant's statements today—the idea of warning the countries that closed their doors to those who were being persecuted came too late, thereby abandoning the victims to their fate. Eichmann said: "In 1939 I set up another central office for emigration in Prague. The Jews were ready to leave and the German authorities were not causing any problems. The main hindrance came from the countries that were to welcome the Jews."

Thursday, June 29

The attitude of Italian authorities who were "sabotaging" the deportations of the Jews from occupied France and Greece was at the center of today's hearing. It appears that the Italian government had protested to Premier Pierre Laval regarding measures taken against non-French Jews. A report sent to the head of the Gestapo, Heinrich Müller, stated: "This will make it impossible to implement our Jewish policy and we will no longer be able to deport the French Jews." The situation became so serious that Müller decided to discuss the matter in Rome in April 1943. Prior to his trip a memorandum had been drafted based upon a conversation with Eichmann summing up the complaints of the RSHA that defined the Italian attitude as "an insurmountable barrier to the Führer's directives."

Judge Ravèh asked who the author of the memorandum was. Eichmann is forced to admit that he had written it but, as usual, "under orders from his superiors." Scores of deportation orders from France and Belgium bear the defendant's signature; telegrams and reports were addressed to him. Eichmann keeps on repeating in a dull voice: "I was only following orders from my superiors."

Friday, June 30

The trial didn't provide a single dramatic event today. We were surprised, however, by a new tack used by the defense: rather than the long disquisitions Eichmann was in the habit of giving us, he simply stated that the most incriminating documents were false. Proof of their falsehood is provided by the perfection of the Nazi bureaucratic machine. Orders to execute by shooting went beyond his area of responsibility; therefore, Eichmann didn't issue them. He doesn't even have any doubts that the judges might believe papers bearing his signature rather than the denials he is offering today.

The fate of 1,200 Serbian Jews is being discussed in September 1941. Franz Rademacher was giving his report to Martin Luther at the Ministry of Foreign Affairs when he got a phone call: "Shoot them!" yelled Eichmann twice and then hung up the phone. This information is contained in a handwritten note on the margins of a document by Rademacher. Eichmann denies everything. "I never made that proposal. I was not competent to issue such orders. Furthermore, our bureaucracy was so well organized that such an important matter wouldn't have been handled over the phone. But most of all, if Rademacher was taking quick notes over the telephone, why would he write so ceremoniously '*Sturmbannführer* Eichmann of IV D6 proposes that…?'" (At the time Eichmann was IV D6.)

Whether it was Serbia, Denmark, or Holland, Eichmann's defense remains unchanged. He steadfastly denies and shifts all responsibility to the Ministry of Foreign Affairs, the army, or his superiors. Servatius introduces a document that states that Eichmann favored the deportation of the Dutch Jews.

"The document has a number of flaws," says Eichmann, "and I gave it a critical examination. The date of 19 September 1941 is used while the Wannsee Conference where deportations were first discussed took place, as you know, on 20 January 1942. Besides, the addressee and the signature are missing; therefore, it is not authentic."

The prosecution had introduced this document to show that Eichmann had been involved in deportations before the Wannsee Conference, but that purpose seems to have eluded the defendant.

Monday, July 3

Eichmann's testimony, now entering its third week, will be interrupted tomorrow by the depositions taken by the commission abroad. The documents shown today to the former SS colonel by his defense lawyer concern the persecutions in Romania, Greece, Bulgaria, Slovakia, Hungary, and Italy.

Following the raid in Rome on October 16, 1943, the German ambassador to the Holy See told Eichmann that a reaction by the Vatican was feared. "Why was Eichmann involved?" asked the chief justice. Eichmann responded: "Because I had to transmit the report to Müller in Berlin asking for instructions, as usual."

In September 1943 Eichmann sent one of his deputies to Greece with orders to deport all the Jews to Auschwitz. Today, Eichmann says he did not issue the order but, when pressed by Chief Judge Landau, he becomes absentminded: "Many years have gone by, Your Honor; I really wouldn't know... It may be that I only sent the order I had received from Müller, my commanding officer."

Acting on Eichmann's behalf in early 1943 in Bulgaria, Theo Dannecker phoned his boss to confirm the agreement he had reached with Bulgarian authorities for the deportation of 20,000 Jews from Thrace and Macedonia. Eichmann cannot deny having received the phone report but he claims that "it came to him, obviously, so that he could pass it along to his superiors and enter into agreements with the railroads."

He had his emissaries in every country: Wisliceny in Greece and Slovakia, then in Hungary where he joined Eichmann; Dannecker in Bulgaria and Italy; Richter in Romania. They were acting as councilors at the local embassies but sent their reports directly to Eichmann. Why? As he explains it should be obvious: "Only to coordinate train schedules." It was an international organization of human transport for the crematoriums. But Eichmann never mentions the destination.

Even in a massacre a certain order must be maintained. Eichmann therefore threatened to take "police measures," such as closing the border if the Romanian authorities continued their "illegal" deportations beyond the river Bug. It is as if he were saying: "Keep on killing your Jews, but do so in an orderly fashion and where we want you to do so."

Eichmann was threatening police action and ordered three railroad cars added to every convoy of deportees out of Holland, while issuing orders for deportation from Greece—all as a simple "transportation official…"

He made his mark even in Slovakia. On March 13, 1942, his visit to Presbourg was announced with plans to deport 20,000 Slovakian Jews. On March 29 the German minister to Bratislava, Hanns Ludin, reported that three trains of deportees had already left. Eichmann commented: "I certainly did prepare those deportations from my office in Berlin."

What efficiency! In less than two weeks, after a quick local inspection Eichmann organized everything from his desk. On its end the Slovak government was providing the "rolling stock" and paying 500 marks per deportee. Certain pleasures must be paid for!

In 1944 Monsignor Joseph Tiso, president of the Slovak State, was worrying about pressure from foreign countries because of the deportation of the Jews. "Tell them that it is the Reich that is demanding a radical solution," suggested German minister Ludin. However, in Berlin von Thadden offered a more diplomatic and more appropriate response for propaganda purposes. The Slovaks were to respond that "Jewish participation in partisan activities requires a radical solution to the Jewish problem." The image of the Jew as a revolutionary is not very original but is always effective. This was the excuse given also at the start of 1945 to the proposal by Dunant, the representative of the International Red Cross, to create a hospice for the aged, children, and sick people: "It could once again become a focus of resistance." The

Nazis were very much afraid of children! Eichmann obviously can't remember this, having given a negative answer, but clearly it could not have come at his own initiative. One may ask if he ever took any kind of initiative as a man constantly protected by a wall of red tape.

Tuesday, July 4

Eichmann remained silent today as the depositions by former Nazis, who had not received immunity in Israel, were being read, since they testified to the commission abroad in order to avoid trial themselves.

The sworn statements by Eichmann's former comrades-in-arms contain many specific accusations against him.

Wilhelm Höttl, who is today the headmaster of a high school in Austria and a former German counterespionage agent, met Eichmann in 1938 in Vienna. He saw him again after the fall of the front in Romania and asked about the actions against the Jews in particular.

"In August 1944 Eichmann came to see me in my apartment in Budapest to ask what I knew about the situation at the front following the coup d'état in Romania and the collapse of the Romanian front. I had rather accurate information, thanks to the intelligence service and the listening posts I had set up in Hungary. Eichmann was very nervous and drank a lot of cognac. Then he got up to take his leave and said: 'We will never see one another again. I know that the Allies consider me a major war criminal, given my tasks in the extermination of the Jews.' I was surprised and asked him for details. 'The number of those killed is a Reich state secret, but you are an historian and I will tell you that up to now six million Jews have been killed, of which four million died in the extermination camps, and two million were shot or killed because of disease.' I was amazed but Eichmann added that according to Himmler the numbers should have been higher. Eichmann showed no guilt feelings; he had simply answered my question." Höttl then called Eichmann "death's greatest freight forwarder." Former SS lieutenant Horst Grell, who reported a similar statement from Eichmann: "I know I am considered to be a war criminal because I killed six million enemies of the Reich."

Von Thadden, the former head of Jewish Affairs at the Ministry of Foreign Affairs, was in constant contact with the defendant and said: "Even if the undersecretary and the minister of foreign affairs himself were to step in, it was impossible to get around Eichmann. He had to be consulted on every issue regarding the Jews. Eichmann was tough and made no exceptions."

Hans Jüttner is a former SS general. In 1944 he saw the columns of Hungarian Jews marching on foot on the Vienna-to-Budapest highway toward the Austrian border. There were hundreds of dead along the road. He was so shaken by this that once he reached Budapest he went to the local SS commander to request an explanation. The commander answered, "Yes I know about it but there's nothing I can do. The march was ordered by Eichmann, who gets his orders directly from Berlin."

Kurt Becher is today a rich German merchant and was a close deputy of Eichmann's at Budapest. Kastner testified in his favor at Nuremberg. He recalled in his deposition the well-known barter— "supplies for blood"—in the exchange of ten thousand trucks for one million Jews. Becher went to see Himmler to negotiate the matter and was told: "Get everything you can from the Jews. We shall see about keeping our promises." But Eichmann was sabotaging the agreement and Himmler called him in Becher's presence. At one point Himmler screamed at Eichmann: "If until now you have exterminated the Jews, henceforth I am ordering you to take care of them! I'm the one giving orders, not Müller and not you!" But Eichmann kept on thwarting every rescue plan, Becher added, and he described him as "a pure nationalist and a fanatical anti-Semite."

Becher claimed that he got Himmler to interrupt the deportation but Himmler feared that Kaltenbrunner would denounce him to the Führer for his efforts.

Wednesday, July 5

Today Eichmann is again testifying about Hungary: this was the only country for which he left his desk in Berlin to handle personally. The crushing testimony of his former colleagues has somewhat diminished his self-assurance and it was natural that he would begin with a blistering attack on former SS colonel Kurt Becher, whose external deposition was read to the court yesterday. Becher claims to have been the one to propose the well-known "supplies for blood" deal to Himmler while Eichmann was doing everything he could to sabotage any rescue attempt.

Right now Eichmann is giving an altogether different explanation. He replies: "Becher was supposed to pick up machinery in Hungary. Why would he be involved in Jewish emigration, an issue where I was the expert? I was steeped in those problems of Jewish emigration!" Besides Becher, the Ministry of Foreign Affairs also got involved in Jewish matters. While other officials busied themselves in what was his area of expertise, Eichmann was relegated to handling those annoying emigration problems. Stung in his professional pride, he wanted a proposal of his own to compete with those of German counterespionage and Becher. To make his plan acceptable he offered to exchange one million Jews. "I couldn't go to Müller to discuss 100,000 Jews or invoke pity," he added. Himmler approved the plan that would equip two divisions and Eichmann sent Joel Brand to Turkey to handle the matter. "I am happy that Brand testified here on how things actually took place. But I didn't promise to destroy the gas chambers at Auschwitz. This was impossible since it didn't belong to my sphere of responsibility."

Eichmann admits having issued the order to the Hungarian gendarmerie to have 50,000 Jews set off on the infamous "death march," and to have been in charge of deportations from Hungary, he also wanted to appear in the eyes of the judges as the only initiator of a serious rescue plan. He only found out about the reasons for the plan's failure during this trial.

Thursday, July 6

"I never killed anyone. I never beat anyone," said Eichmann this morning at the start of the hearing as he was commenting on testimony that he had murdered a Jewish boy in the garden of his villa in Budapest in 1944. "I am not saying that the witness swore to something false, but I really have no idea where this information could have come from. I had a very active social life and yet no one ever brought up that incident and it is only now, in 1961, that the matter is being brought up," he added.

Other than outright denials, Eichmann admits some of the things he is accused of, but always because of orders coming from higher up. "Toward the end of 1941 Müller sent me on an inspection of various locations. I went to Lublin, where the exhaust fumes of an old engine were being used to kill the Jews. In Minsk I saw the mass shooting of the Jews in a common pit. I think it is rather easy to figure out the date of my visit because I recall wearing a leather jacket on that occasion. Therefore it had to be during the winter." As usual his main worry is to make sure that the dates are right or that the smallest details of his uniform are correct. "In Auschwitz I saw the corpses being cremated on large iron grids. But my task was only to be present, to keep my eyes open, take notes, and report back to my superiors without adding any comments. It is not true that Höss, as he wrote in his book, consulted me about using gas for exterminations. That was none of my business.

"In August 1942, as I was taking the order to kill between 150 and 250,000 Jews to Globocnik in Lublin, I went by Lvov, where for the first time I saw a fountain of blood. They had shot some Jews and had thrown them in a pit too quickly. Because of the gases, blood was shooting up from the earth like a fountain. But I can't remember if it was October 22 or 23. I took those trips against my will. I had orders and followed them. I have nothing to add."

The file for the super bureaucrat Eichmann is closed, and that is the only thing that interests him.

He went on: "I asked for a transfer many times but I had to execute the orders coming from my superiors. All this had to happen to someone like me, who until then had only been involved in the plans for Madagascar and had never even considered a bloody or violent solution!"

Friday, July 7

Today Eichmann put the final touches on his self-portrait as he concluded his testimony with his Nazi "belief system."

"I must make a difference between the legal and the human aspect," he said. "The deportations were the responsibility of those making political decisions. Where there is no responsibility there can be no guilt. In order to protect its security the State ties the individual to an oath; issues of conscience belong to the sovereign, the head of state. I was not lucky and my head of state issued the orders for deportations to take place. My role was assigned to me by the commander of the SS and police whose orders I received through his subordinates. I did everything I could to be transferred but didn't succeed and was compelled to obey. I was in uniform and there was a war going on. My task was the most difficult of all but I had to see it through. For cases of insubordination the SS penal code provided death as punishment. One could commit suicide but couldn't oppose his orders. Today I do feel sorry and condemn the extermination of the Jews as ordered by the German leaders, but I was only an instrument in their hands and also in the hands of a fate that knew no mercy."

With these words Eichmann has ended his testimony. Chief prosecutor Hausner then began his cross-examination. Standing up, now without his documents and hammered with questions that forced him to improvise with short, clear answers, Eichmann lost much of his self-assurance and conceit.

The prosecutor asked him: "In the course of the pre-trial examination you stated: 'I know that I shall be considered as an accomplice to the murders. I know that I can be condemned to death and ask for no mercy because I don't deserve it.' You then added that you would be ready to hang yourself in public to pay for your awful crimes. Are you ready to repeat this now and confirm it?"

Eichmann: "Yes, I don't deny it."

Hausner: "So you therefore confess to having been an accomplice in the murder of millions of Jews?"

Eichmann: "No, I cannot confess to that. I do not consider myself guilty from the legal point of view since I was executing orders; however from the human point of view, yes, for having carried out the deportations."

Monday, July 10

The cross-examination that began last Friday has deeply upset Eichmann. This morning the court agreed to the defense's request to suspend the morning hearing since Eichmann had a sleepless night and appeared to be nervous and exhausted. As is customary for royal families, a medical bulletin was issued shortly after: following a careful examination the police doctor stated that Eichmann was in excellent health and was only tired because of his lack of sleep he had been experiencing. Finally, the cold mask of the impassive man has fallen; today we found out what it cost him to maintain it until now. Perhaps the biting and ironic questioning by the prosecutor has brought the certainty of the day of judgment closer. Is it the memory of all those corpses that is interfering with his sleep? That seems hard to believe. It's more likely to be the shadow of the gallows.

During this afternoon's hearing Eichmann, under the rapid fire of direct cross-examination, resembled an insect caught in the web that was being woven slowly around him. Often he shutters himself behind convenient lapses of memory. "What can I say, Mr. Prosecutor? After twenty-four years I don't remember some of the details..." He cannot even remember whether or not Dannecker was one of his staff members in 1940. On the other hand, the documents can always be helpful; Eichmann desperately attempts to hang on to them and from time to time the court is forced to listen to his tortuous answers to questions that offer only one other possibility: is it true, yes or no, that you issued such and such an order?

The afternoon hearing concerned the initial period of Eichmann's activity in 1938–39. To the prosecutor's question as to whether he was aware of the Nazi slogans of "Death to the Jews" when he joined the party, the defendant answered: "I joined the party to fight against the Treaty of Versailles, even though for the most part I later fought against Judaism. The Jews had to be destroyed since their leader Weizmann had declared war on Germany. The Führer had also said so in one of his speeches. But I wasn't thinking of physical extermination. When we mentioned the destruction of our enemies such as France and England, we only wanted to make them harmless." The prosecutor then countered: "But Dr. Weizmann never issued such a declaration of war!" Eichmann answered: "I wouldn't know, I can only repeat what was being said at the time."

The cross-examination continued while the prosecutor referred back to Eichmann's statements during the pre-trial statement that the defendant claims not to remember. At times he is forced to minimize or at times to contradict himself. Hausner insisted: "In other words, summing it up, one may say that your office was responsible for all Jewish life in the Reich, including welfare assistance?" "No, absolutely not," answered Eichmann. "The documents indicate that only the head of Office IV was making important decisions."

We are back to the usual devices; Eichmann once more is hanging on to his beloved documents. But the way they are used by the prosecutor they appear to contradict Eichmann and many times in the course of the hearing he was forced to deny what he had previously stated, denying all the compromising statements he made during the pre-trial examination.

Tuesday, July 11

The pressing questions asked by the prosecutor continued today with his cross-examination and his forcing Eichmann to admit some key points.

Eichmann said that he hadn't been the only one handling Jewish issues; they were also the purview of other departments as well.

"Yes," said the prosecutor, "we are well aware that you couldn't have killed six million Jews all by yourself. You obviously had to work with other sections. But both Heydrich and Kaltenbrunner, his successor, referred to you as 'our expert for Jewish questions.'"

Eichmann had to add that he was the only one in the Reich Main Security Office (RSHA) to have the title of "Officer of Jewish Affairs." An even more important admission was probably that all letters bearing his signature, whether written under the orders of his commander or on his—Eichmann's—personal initiative, were, in accordance with regulations inside the Gestapo, to carry the words "*im auftrage,*" meaning "in the name of." Until now, when facing documents with his signature, the former SS colonel had often used that formula to prove that he only transmitted letters that had really been written by his chiefs.

By the end of the day the prosecution was able to make some headway but was unable to break Eichmann, who continues to deny even the clearest evidence with his own brand of logic.

Wednesday, July 12

"They all lied" was Eichmann's comment upon hearing the statements of many former SS officers who said that he had a particularly important position as the main expert for the deportation of the Jews, and as such that he was responsible for their execution.

Documents indicate that the German Ministry of Foreign Affairs consulted with Eichmann for the demands to be made with Mussolini; in Denmark it was again Eichmann who was issuing orders on behalf of the RSHA. "These are clumsy mistakes due to the total ignorance and bureaucratic negligence of those offices," says Eichmann. "I was only an intermediary."

The prosecutor asked: "But then how do you explain your dogged opposition to prevent even individual Jews from escaping death? Max Golon tried to escape to Switzerland. Nobody came to you about that. Why did you step in to block his flight?"

"I received orders and had to fulfill them in spite of my reluctance," is Eichmann's inevitable answer.

"But then Hitler was the only one who was guilty?"

"No, Himmler and Kaltenbrunner were guilty, since they had a certain amount of veto power. But the subordinates like myself could only obey."

The prosecutor then quotes from a section of the memoir that Eichmann had dictated to Sassen in 1957. "When I was given the order to fight the Jews I acted with the greatest degree of fanaticism, like an old Nazi. I could say that I was bound by my oath. But that would be idle gossip. I did the best I could to understand what I was doing since fate had endowed me with personal characteristics that were particularly effective for that task. I wasn't just a low-level person simply carrying out orders; I would have been an idiot. I thought my orders through and participated in their implementation because I was an idealist."

Eichmann stutters as he replies: "I can't imagine having said that. The memoir includes both the truth and falsehood since I was often drunk."

"So then, are you an idiot or an idealist?"

"No, I was thinking… I was not an idiot but I was an idealist."

Torn between the desire to appear important and the hope of saving his own skin, Eichmann is unable to decide which role to pick. He is following a pre-established defense strategy, according to which the entire responsibility will fall on his superiors. But it is exactly the principle of non-responsibility that the prosecutor has been trying to undermine today. By his monotonous answers, his arrogance, and even his aggressive responses, not only did Eichmann handle Hausner's cross-examination very well but he also seems to have managed to have exhausted him. Hausner, on the other hand, has often skipped the necessary delay for the translation from Hebrew to German that makes any dialogue cumbersome and was addressing the defendant directly in German.

Thursday, July 13

"I must say that I view the murder of the Jews to be one of the greatest crimes in all human history."

Eichmann made this sensational statement this morning after dodging an answer to the specific question by the prosecutor: "Do you consider that someone who was handling the extermination of the Jews, like Höss in Auschwitz, to be a criminal? Yes or no?" At first Eichmann preferred to not answer; then he said he thought Höss was an unfortunate man and that in any case he is under no obligation to convey his personal feelings to the court. He also added that had he been responsible for the extermination he would have committed suicide, since at that time he already considered the violent solution to be both indefensible and illegal. "My contribution came in the form of transportation, because I had sworn allegiance to the flag. But having left all the decisions to my superiors I could consider myself innocent and be at peace with myself."

To the prosecutor's question about his knowledge of the use of gas, Eichmann answered: "Yes, I did know something about the business of gas… But I can't remember it too well. I feel very confused. I got into a violent argument with Günther, my deputy, because he got involved in the matter. I was clearly thinking about 'Zyklon-B' because I had seen what was going on with that gas in the east. But Günther must have received a direct order from Müller behind my back and I can certainly not be held responsible."

Rudolf Höss, in his book *Commandant at Auschwitz*, wrote, among other things, that Eichmann had a free hand in the attack on the Jews and that since he had doubts about a German victory he was pressuring everyone to act radically and as quickly as possible. Eichmann, who in 1957 had called Höss "a dear friend," was entirely predictable: "It is a complete travesty of the truth… I was only following orders from my superior."

"So, you where just a small-time messenger?" asked the prosecutor. "Yes, that's exactly right." The audience laughs and Eichmann, stung in his pride, jumps to his feet and corrects himself: "Not really a messenger, but rather a German officer conveying secret orders."

"Why then did Müller, your commanding officer, say: 'Had we had fifty Eichmanns we would have won the war?'"

"I always did my duty. Perhaps Müller meant that everyone should have been just as dedicated as public officials."

Eichmann always has a ready answer to every accusation, even if it's not very convincing. The cross-examination doesn't manage to pin him down with his crushing responsibility nor does it force him to make a full confession.

Friday, July 14

Today Eichmann admitted to traveling to the Italian occupation sector in France in the course of one of his many inspection trips in various European countries. But this was only to transmit orders issued by his superiors.

"So then, all they did was give you letters to write like a menial typist?" asks the prosecutor.

"No, it's obvious that I didn't have to consult my chiefs for every letter. But Müller was the one who would make key decisions and at times he would have Himmler himself decide." "You mean to say that in the end it was Hitler who decided everything in the Third Reich?" The prosecutor insisted: "Why then did you always write in the first person: I have decided, I order, my office in Paris, in Oslo…?"

"I regret that I must always give a negative answer and say: I wasn't the one. But that is the way it was even though I can't prove it since most of the German archives have been destroyed."

"Yes. However, many witnesses are still alive. When you issued orders to deport 90,000 Jews from France, Belgium, and Holland to Auschwitz, were you not aware that they were headed to the gas chambers?"

"Yes, I could imagine as much."

Then he adds in a blank voice: "But I was conveying orders."

"But if you were only a low-level bureaucrat," adds the prosecutor, "how was it that you were writing to the Ministry of Foreign Affairs that you only wanted to deport Jews able to work out of Romania while you were telling Himmler on the same day that sick Jews were to be added to the convoys? The German Ministry of Foreign Affairs clearly played its part in the massacre but you tried to hoodwink them by hiding parts of the measures being taken against the Jews."

"Those were Himmler's orders—"

"No, that's not true," the prosecutor cuts in, "because Himmler sent a copy of your letter to the Ministry of Foreign Affairs which got Killinger quite angry when he was critical in referring to 'Eichmann's well-known methods.' Is that not true?"

"I must conclude that someone in Himmler's office made a mistake," answers the defendant.

The pattern continues the same as before: Eichmann is busy every day discovering new inefficiencies in the perfect Nazi bureaucracy, and that appears to be his sole concern.

Monday, July 17

Eichmann didn't limit his deportations to the Jews. Poles, Gypsies, and Slovenes were also included. He admitted this morning that he had deported over half a million Poles to Auschwitz in order to Germanize the Zamosz region in accordance with Himmler's orders as the "Reich High Commissioner for the settlement of the German People."

"Prior to my becoming involved there was nothing but anarchy in transportation, an enormous chaos with people remaining locked up in the boxcars for as many as eight days. I was brought in to put an end to all that."

For the umpteenth time Eichmann repeated that he never took any initiative and limited himself to asking Müller for instructions. The prosecutor then goes back to a question he had asked previously: "Why is it then that Müller stated that with fifty Eichmanns he would have won the war?"

"He was referring to my action in shutting off fire bombs," Eichmann answered quietly. Judge Halevy added: "But in that case you were a poor official since you were not fully using your authority."

Stung in his pride Eichmann answers: "That's not true. I was always loyal to my oath."

The prosecutor then asked: "Here is an order you signed to hang some Jews in public inside the ghetto. How many such orders did you issue?"

"I don't know, I can't remember... I was only transmitting Himmler's orders."

Upon returning from a trip to the east, Eichmann told his commanding officer Müller that the shootings had to end and that a more elegant way must be found, otherwise the soldiers involved in the executions would risk becoming sadists. Eichmann admitted proposing the use of gas but then denied it and said that the document introduced by the prosecution on the subject was false. In the memoir he had dictated to Sassen, Eichmann had written: "We had to avoid having the brains of a Jewish child soil the leather jacket of a German soldier."

To the question from the prosecutor as to why he traveled to Warsaw before and after the ghetto uprising, Eichmann replied: "I happened to be passing through Warsaw. I stopped there because it was the most convenient place to spend the night."

The morning session was interrupted by a brief incident: an old man suddenly got up and waved his arm bearing the tattoo of his number as a deportee while he yelled out insults at the defendant.

Tuesday, July 18

For the first time since the beginning of the trial Eichmann came out of his glass booth to indicate on a map with a pointer, just like a school teacher, which territories were not part of his jurisdiction.

Today the trial has gone beyond the 100th day; Eichmann's cross-examination is proceeding in a cumbersome manner, so much so that Judge Landau told the prosecutor that the current portion of the trial had to end.

Eichmann admitted knowing about the situation in the concentration camps of Bergen Belsen and Theresienstadt. In the latter, which was considered as having national importance, Eichmann in the course of an inspection even worried about the way the beds were lined up.

The prosecutor asked the defendant which law gave an extermination camp commandant the right to murder the deportees. "No such law actually existed. I was not involved in such matters but I do know that orders from the Führer had the same value as law," answered Eichmann.

"But the deportations you made were based on a Reich law, or were they not?"

"I am not a legal expert, and the legal basis of our actions was of no interest to me. I would receive orders and I would carry them out."

The prosecutor then recalled the deportation of the children of Lidice, the Czech village subjected to the Nazi reprisals for the murder of Reinhard Heydrich, who was Eichmann's commanding officer. Krumey had phoned from Poland asking Eichmann what he should do with the 88 children from Lidice. "Why did he ask Eichmann?" asked the prosecutor.

"I really wouldn't know," Eichmann answered. "Obviously he made a mistake. He didn't know who was in charge. On the other hand, Krumey is under arrest. Why not ask him?

"Actually your deputy Günther did give Krumey an answer; did he do so behind your back?" asked the prosecutor.

"Yes, he obviously did. Müller may have given him direct orders," was the defendant's answer.

Eichmann stuck to this absurd position even regarding the matter of collecting Jewish skeletons that had been requested by the University of Strasbourg. He had to have received the request, which was addressed to him, but then he passed it on to Müller, who put Günther in charge without telling Eichmann. The defendant considers this to be a logical bureaucratic procedure.

Wednesday, July 19

Eichmann is about to become an expert in the art of impersonation right in front of our eyes. Today the prosecution introduced a letter from Heydrich where it is stated that: "My division head Eichmann called for a meeting in his office about sterilization." According to the minutes there were three other officials besides Eichmann taking part in that meeting. But this doesn't prove that he was involved in sterilizations. "We had no further space we could use, so our offices were often used for meetings. The participation by four IV B4 officials was certainly useless but everyone was happy to drop their boring job for a while to discuss more interesting topics."

The chief justice finds it necessary to interrupt the defendant's tortuous replies: "Your answers are truly intolerable. You must absolutely be more concise!"

The prosecutor then moves on to Eichmann's activities in Hungary, the only country where he acted directly beyond his office in Berlin. At the time Himmler had said: "I am sending the boss himself to Hungary to make sure the Jews don't revolt as they did in the Warsaw ghetto." Today Eichmann denied having heard those words, even though that is what he told Sassen in his memoir, and he further denies playing an important part in rounding up the Jews in Hungary. "I handled only the technical side; my men were present as the convoys got under way only in order to withdraw the Jews of foreign nationality in accordance with the orders from the German ambassador in Budapest. The Hungarian gendarmerie was in charge of the convoys to Auschwitz and I could only set up the schedules and ask for confirmation of the arrival of each train."

"But then," asked the prosecutor, "if you really were only a low-level official who never took any initiatives, how could you even dare offer one million Jews in exchange for 10,000 trucks?"

"I wanted to take the plans for Jewish emigration, which had always been my specialty, out of Becher's hands. I admit that my initiative was motivated more by opportunism than by the desire to save some Jews."

Thursday, July 20

During the final moments of today's hearing, the Eichmann trial took a radical turn. Judge Raveh finally moved the focus of the debate away from the documents, where it had become bogged down, to focus on the moral level, which is the only valid level in the case. Eichmann was forced to admit that he had acted against the dictates of his own conscience. With just a few questions Judge Raveh was able to obtain perhaps far more than the prosecutor, who in two weeks hadn't managed to extract much more than some minor admissions from the defendant.

"In the course of the examination before trial, you stated that you always tried to live according to the Kantian imperative. Did this also apply to the time when you were deporting the Jews to the death camps?" asked Raveh.

"No, because killing is contrary to the laws of God and therefore to the Kantian imperative as well. But I was not free to act as I pleased. I had to obey and with the little I knew of the Kantian imperative it had only one meaning: to obey the laws. I was reading Kant while I was traveling and he is not that clear to me, even today. When I visited the Chelmno camp I understood that I couldn't follow those principles and that I had to adapt to the circumstances. So then I got into the habit of always turning to Müller and transferring every responsibility to him."

Before he ended his cross-examination the prosecutor again used the efficient weapon of the memoir that Eichmann dictated to Sassen, where the tragic march of the Hungarian Jews to Vienna was clearly set up by the defendant. "I wanted to make the point that deportations could continue even when the rails were bombed." As Eichmann wrote: "I therefore sent out a first group of 10,000 Jews on foot. A few days later the Hungarian undersecretary Endre congratulated me for the success of that elegant operation and we drank to that together, with satisfaction."

Eichmann also admitted having inspected the Auschwitz death camp at that time to confirm that it could accommodate the new arrivals. In the afternoon, after the prosecutor and before the judges, defense attorney Servatius again took the floor to ask his client to provide a few explanations.

Friday, July 21

Today the judges continued to question the defendant. While answering a question from Judge Raveh, who was asking him in German about how his department was set up, Eichmann admitted that he had always known about the actions taken by those under his command. He would send Müller their reports but wouldn't add a single comment or make any suggestions. "I know this may sound strange but everyone had something to say about Jewish issues and not even Müller could make any proposals since we were already getting so many from the outside."

Raveh: "During the examination before trial you stated that you couldn't wash your hands of the killings that had taken place."

Eichmann: "It's clear to me today that the fact of having been given orders is meaningless. But if I think of how many times I tried to obtain a different job and the fact that I had attempted to avoid being transferred to Berlin, I can say that I did what I could and that I am not guilty. I was only the instrument of stronger forces."

Then it was Judge Halevy's turn. He questioned the defendant in German as well: "You have stated several times your wish that the whole truth be known about yourself. If that is indeed the case then we share a common goal. This is an objective court but it is not naïve. Today you are given perhaps your last opportunity to tell the world the truth. Remember that." He went on: "Even if there had been a declaration of war by the Jewish people on Germany, why did you treat the Jewish people in an altogether different way from your other enemies?"

Eichmann: "Yes, I admit that to be the case. We were following Hitler's racial theory."

Halevy: "Were you personally an anti-Semite?"

Eichmann: "No, certainly not. But to be uncompromising was a virtue, especially following Himmler's speech when he demanded that SS officers cleanse Germany of the Jews without any exceptions."

Halevy: "You were never bothered by your conscience? You never felt any conflict between duty and morality?"

Eichmann: "I chose the path dictated by the circumstances. Any other position would have appeared to be insubordination and I don't know what would have happened to me. Today I wonder why such large segments of the population lacked civic courage and why the authorities were able to act so brutally. Perhaps everyone was thinking that any kind of individual revolt would have been useless. From the human point of view it is clear that I have already passed judgment on my actions. However, both the massacres of Jews and the atomic bombs are both crimes against humanity that at the time were considered to be legal by the top leadership."

Monday, July 24

Eichmann's cross-examination, the longest in Israeli judicial history, ended this morning. The court's presiding judge, Landau, said, as he addressed the defendant, "You have stated that you never were an anti-Semite. This sounds very odd for a Nazi true believer who certainly had to be reading the propaganda against the Jews in the party's mouthpiece, the *Völkischer Beobachter*."

Eichmann replied: "Yes Mr. President, it may appear to be a paradox. But I would read the newspaper at a café or in the office and we simple employees were more interested in the national economic misery than in abstract issues. My personal interests at the time were not about literature or other spiritual values. After I was transferred to the Reich Main Security Office [RSHA] I was deeply immersed in my files and was only concerned about possibly being transferred to a position that didn't fit my qualifications. In other words I was not a hard liner."

"But why then didn't Müller dismiss you from your job? And why didn't you request to be sent to the front?" asked the chief justice.

"I wouldn't know; it would certainly have been a great help to me. But I was very accurate in my work and carried out orders scrupulously. So that may be the reason why Müller took a liking to me. He was also extremely detail-oriented and didn't make decisions on his own initiative."

Eichmann then described the Wannsee Conference once more, saying: "Everyone was openly discussing the methods of extermination: shootings and the exhaust fumes of diesel engines. The atmosphere was relaxed and the orderlies were serving cognac and other drinks. Heydrich then asked me to draft the minutes of the meeting, underlining the participation of the secretaries of state in order to create a retroactive alibi by having them carry all responsibility."

The prosecutor spoke briefly to ask: "You stated that you couldn't live according to Kant's categorical imperative during the war because you were subjected to the will of a far more powerful force. But then is tearing the Gospel away from your wife while she was reading it part of the categorical imperative?"

Eichmann could do no better than to stutter for an answer: "I am certainly not infallible and you cannot always live your private life according to your principles."

Defense attorney Servatius then introduced the depositions collected by the commission traveling abroad—some ten statements in all that didn't provide any decisive elements. One of them concerns Herbert Kappler, who was testifying from his prison cell in Gaeta. He states that the October 16, 1943, raid on the Jews in Rome was organized by SS captain Dannecker. As it had been testified to earlier, Dannecker reported directly to Eichmann.

This is a brief summary of Kappler's deposition: "I can't remember who first gave me the order to proceed with the raid and the deportation of the Jews in Rome. I do remember very well, however, that I never was ordered to round up and deport a specific number of Jews. It stated only 'the Jews of Rome.'

"I remember that an SS captain named Dannecker came to the office with full powers and an authorization to proceed with the rounding-up of the Jews, ordering local police commanders to provide all the assistance he would require. When the order for the raid was given to me, I was angry at the lack of understanding on the part of the top commanders who had issued illogical and damaging orders from a political point of view. I remember writing to those who were in a position to help me in my efforts to avoid what I thought to be *eine neue gross politische Dummheit*, another big political blunder.

"I can say very little about how the raid was carried out and the final destination of those being deported.

"The operation was organized and carried out by Captain Dannecker, who as I said came to Rome with a dozen men and discretionary powers that Müller had provided. Three companies of the *Ordnungspolizei* were dispatched to Rome out of nowhere in expectation of the operation. These three companies were under Dannecker's orders. To begin with, I told him that I had no men to place at his disposal. When he asked me about the topographic information to set up the operational plan, I told him that I didn't have any people with good knowledge of the city and that he should contact the Italian police headquarters.

"I knew that through the Italian police the information would have reached the Jews, who could then save themselves.

"Later on Dannecker told me that he had all the information he required.

"He showed me a little box with many envelopes and told me that each patrol had a very specific task in certain houses and buildings. He said he also had the names and addresses of the Jews. I remember that he extracted one envelope from the collection and to prove to me the perfection of his organization he showed me its contents.

"I recall that to avoid revealing the raid, Dannecker had initially preferred to hold the Italian policemen in the German barracks. I couldn't stop this, but after a few days using as an excuse the lack of food supplies, I ended the confinement of the Italian officers. Thus I broke the secrecy that Dannecker had enforced so well. Following the raid I was told that the Jews were on a train,` ready to leave without any food. I rushed to the Ministry of the Interior to plead for them and Prefect Testa promised me that he would do something.

"No one gave me orders to demand 50 kilos of gold from the Jews of Rome. That was my final attempt to try and avoid the raid that Dannecker was about to undertake. I remember that it was an emergency decision that I took once he told me that the raid was about to begin and that without some new element that could change things dramatically, the order would inevitably be carried out. I am still convinced today that if a whole series of unfortunate events hadn't taken place, and most of all had Kaltenbrunner been in Berlin when I transmitted the information regarding my attempt and when I shipped the gold, the raid could have been avoided. I asked for the gold as a voluntary gesture.

"I contacted Kaltenbrunner because until then he hadn't been involved in all the discussions regarding the advisability of undertaking the raid in Rome and because he was responsible for the intelligence service. I also wanted him to understand that by putting the Jews in prison or by deporting them we would lose an excellent source of financing for our espionage organization by taking advantage of the existing relationships between the Jewish elements in Rome and those of neutral or enemy countries. My idea may have been silly or naïve, but my intentions were precisely to avoid the raid and the deportation.

"The raids against the Jews after October 16 were authorized by the circular letter announcing their arrest by the Italian police, the citizens, and whoever else wanted to do so. I was given the letter through the usual reporting channels but I can't remember who had signed it. It pertained only to Italy and it was obvious that agreements between the two governments had been reached. I recall asking the Rome police chief, whom I had summoned to my office to find out why and with what right he was engaged in a hunt for Jews no matter whether it meant trespassing into extraterritorial offices. He answered that he could do nothing about it since those were the orders he had received. Following that conversation I met with Kesselring and in his name I forbade the Rome police chief from continuing to violate extraterritoriality under any circumstances."

The trial will now be interrupted. In one week the prosecutor will give his final summation and the defense will have the final word. The court will then withdraw to chambers, but a few months will go by before the verdict is read.

Tuesday, July 25

The second and next-to-last phase of the trial dealing with the defense ended this morning with a very short session, after four months of testimony.

During his questioning Eichmann spoke at length, maintaining that he had no responsibility, that he was following orders from higher up, and in effect hadn't been an anti-Semite. Often he dodged, saying: "I don't remember."

This morning the statement of Franz Slawik, Eichmann's orderly and driver in Budapest in 1944, was read into the record, thereby completing the series of notarized testimonies taken abroad. Slawik confirmed what one of the witnesses for the prosecution stated about Eichmann's villa and the digging of air raid shelters. He recalled that one of Eichmann's drivers had been shot by the Nazis because he had killed an old woman. But he could not recall the main point: he couldn't say anything about the Jewish boy killed, "according to that witness," for having stolen cherries in the garden of the villa in Budapest.

The prosecutor requested that other documents be placed on the record, including a calculation setting at two and a half million the number of victims at Auschwitz concentration camp. But the court agreed to the objection by the defense and refused the request, since it came after the term that had been set.

Tuesday, August 8

In a measured and serious voice that was breaking at times under the emotional impact, yet remaining free from rhetoric, prosecutor Gideon Hausner began his final summation today. It was broadcast

live and listened to by thousands of Israelis on local radio. The trial
that had been interrupted for two weeks is now entering its final phase.

"This trial has painted the picture of a regime that was unable to
suppress human freedom. The ghost of Adolf Hitler and of his
acolytes has appeared here and humanity will forever remember them
as the incarnation of evil. The defendant Adolf Eichmann acted and
spoke just like his leader: a liar with a sweet-sounding voice when he
encountered trouble; destructive and evil as soon as he became
successful. The hypocritical attitude hides a murderer lusting for death
whose thirst can never be quenched.

"As early as 1940, even before Hitler's orders for the physical
extermination were issued, Eichmann set up the first deportations to
the east. When we think of the little Renate Alexander, age 5, who fell
frozen to death in the snow near Stettin and of other victims, the
tortuous discussions with the defendant about the origin of this or that
document have no value.

"Eichmann's exceptional memory allowed him to remember the
furniture in his office, the paper he would write on, the cost of a glass
of beer. But he is unable to recall anything about the gas he supplied to
the death camps, nor does he even remember seeing the Jews in the
sealed boxcars.

"As a member of a criminal organization, Eichmann is, according
to Israeli law, fully responsible. He cannot use the excuse of having
acted under the orders of a dictator, as it was clearly established at
Nuremberg and in Israeli law.

"Eichmann was not, as he would have us believe, a small cog in the
Nazi set-up, whose only concern were train schedules. The defendant
is directly responsible for the deportations to the extermination camps
and when he issued those orders he was signing as many death sentences. Eichmann was seeking a more elegant solution than the firing
squads in order to avoid turning the young SS guards into sadists and
he found the 'Zylon-B' gas that he then shipped to the camps.

"No one has ever denied that many other sections of the Reich
took part in the massacre of the Jews, but this doesn't reduce Eichmann's responsibility in any way."

The prosecutor then recalled the scores of witnesses who spoke of cruelty, torture, and almost unbelievable horror. "One of them, Rivka Yosselevska, can serve as a symbol for the entire Jewish people. They wanted to kill her and even though she was wounded she escaped from the pit. They wanted to erase her kind by murdering her family and she gave light to other children. As the prophet said, the dry bones have gained flesh and tendons and a new spirit of life has revived them."

Wednesday, August 9

Continuing with his closing statement, the prosecutor denied Eichmann's excuse that he was only executing orders. He stated that "the laws of man do not accept such an excuse. Blind obedience would have a soldier firing on his colonel if his captain ordered him to do so. During those years Eichmann was well aware of the fact that he was committing crimes and that is the reason why he attempted to cover up the traces. But he was far more than someone just carrying out orders: he was fanatical in directing and overseeing that they were carried out. He persecuted every single Jew trying to save himself. Was every soldier in the firing squads part of the enormous criminal organization? Well, I must answer: yes.

"The former SS colonel had total control over the fate of the Jews deported to Auschwitz; as the camp commandant testified, Eichmann decided which trains were to go to the gas chambers and which ones to the work detail. The defendant was seen inside the camp four or five times; he would appear when another wave of deportations was to begin, because he had full power to start or stop the death mills.

"In Hungary after the Nazi occupation in 1944, Eichmann was given the task of transporting all the Hungarian Jews to the concentration camps since he was their real 'boss.' His attitude toward the leaders of the Jewish community in Budapest was not that of a simple official executing orders but rather was typical of someone who fully identified with his task.

"Eichmann agreed to take on this mission on condition that the camp at Auschwitz would handle the deportees at the pace he had established. Beforehand, he made an inspection tour of the camp for this purpose. In three and a half months the Auschwitz crematoriums, working night and day, burned 447,402 Jews, according to the official Nazi records. Eichmann acted as quickly as possible to preclude any possibility that anyone might save himself, even those who were expecting a permit to emigrate.

"Eichmann was not the initiator of the well-known "blood for trucks"—the exchange of 10,000 trucks for one million Jews. On the contrary, he did his best to make sure that it would fail, and, as he told Sassen, such an idea couldn't have come from his brain."

Thursday, August 10

"Judges of Israel, we do not ask for vengeance. A new Jeremiah would have to appear to cry over our losses. The millions of Jews who were killed cannot be brought back to life; but we do ask that justice be done and I am proud to be able to invoke the law against the one who attempted to butcher our people." With those words the prosecutor ended his closing statement today against Adolf Eichmann.

"Eichmann is guilty," said the prosecutor, "because up to the end he collaborated fanatically and with enthusiasm in the massacre of the Jewish people. He wanted to wipe every trace of Jewish life from the face of the earth. But he didn't limit himself to mass murder. The cruelty of the Auschwitz camp, the humiliations in seeking to erase human dignity, the torture that compelled the prisoners to throw themselves on the electric fence—none of this is any less serious than homicide. But Eichmann is also guilty of crimes committed against all of humanity. As it is described in the fifteen counts of the indictment, he deported Poles and Gypsies and organized the theft of Jewish property, even shaving off hair from the corpses and yanking out the gold teeth.

"As Eichmann stated on the eve of the German surrender, about five million enemies had been killed. But who could the enemies of this colonel be, since he never fired a shot at the front? They were the defenseless ones, the Jews, the only ones he had enough courage to stand up and fight against.

"Eichmann's one regret is that he never managed to complete his task and had to leave a few Jews alive. But that was only because of the advancing Allied and Soviet armies and not due to Eichmann.

"The Nazis wanted to turn back the wheels of civilization. Like Attila, Hitler brought down upon Europe the lash of cruelty and brutality. He completely destroyed cities and villages and killed entire populations. The Jewish people were to be exterminated first, as the victims of a cold calculation, but then other peoples were to have shared the same fate had the Nazis won.

"In the darkness that descended upon Europe a few lights still flickered. The Jewish people, who never forget their enemies, shall never forget those who helped them. We shall remember the Danes and the Swedes, the Dutch, and the French partisans; the Italian officials who made sure that Mussolini's plans would fail; the priests and the Italian people who helped the Jews in such a large measure. We shall also remember that there were also honest Germans in spite of the mass of Nazi criminals."

Today Eichmann listened to the prosecutor's final summation without looking at him and kept his head down. He has at last discarded his pencils and his endless note taking!

The trial will resume next Monday when defense attorney Servatius will give his closing arguments.

Monday, August 14

After four months and 114 sessions the initial phase of the Eichmann trial ended with the closing arguments by his defense attorney, Servatius, who requested that the charges be dropped and that his client be set free.

The closing statement was purposefully brief and Servatius offered his legal arguments in writing.

"Mr. Presiding Judge, if the description given by the prosecution were true, it could form the basis of a monument erected to the enemies of the Jews. Fortunately it is built on sand. The great Nazi criminals would then be innocent because we now have the one guilty official. This is the strange result of this trial. But the truth is different."

In attacking the Israeli law against Nazi crimes, Servatius said that one couldn't take into account the collective guilt of all those belonging to the SS and the SD. He then denied that the court was competent to stand in judgment for crimes committed against the Poles, Slovenes, and gypsies because those crimes took place at a time when the state of Israel didn't yet exist and were not within its borders.

Rejecting each one of the fifteen counts of the indictment, Servatius then said that one cannot talk about war crimes because there was no state of war between Nazi Germany and the then non-existent State of Israel. As for the persecution of the Jews, there is no clear legal definition of the Jewish people, since at the time the crimes were committed the people of the State of Israel didn't exist and therefore no crime could be committed against it.

Further, Servatius defined the extermination by gas and sterilization "a medical issue" and denied that the defendant had any responsibility for the deportations since they took place on the basis of orders from his superiors. Even the setting up of ghettos and work camps were not the defendant's responsibility.

"The many documents introduced by the prosecution are fragmented and give a false picture of the situation. Nor can one use what Eichmann dictated to the newsman Sassen in Argentina because he was under the influence of alcohol and the book had to be sensational to build up its sales.

"As for the main accusation relating to the killings inside the extermination camps, it must first be made clear that those camps were not under Eichmann's orders. He paid visits but went to Auschwitz to help a member of the Vienna Jewish Council, which does not mean that he had special powers within the camp. Even if it were true that Eichmann's deputy provided 'Zyklon B' to the camps, there is no proof that Eichmann knew anything about it.

"The defendant did not occupy an executive position. He always signed under orders from his superior. His decision-making powers were limited even though the prosecutor inflated them by attempting to turn the defendant into the key individual in the extermination.

"This trial shouldn't be a vendetta against the defendant for crimes committed by the political leadership of the State. The trial must be a warning to future generations. The defendant was part of a military organization and had to obey the orders he was given. Even Moses killed when it became necessary for reasons of state. The state demands blind obedience from its citizens and it is that kind of obedience that insures its existence. The defendant could only obey; he tried to get transferred to the front but failed. When the individual acts on the basis of a firm order it is the state that is responsible for the crime and not the individual. International law recognizes the reason of state as a mitigating factor.

"Furthermore, retroactive laws are contrary to generally accepted legal principles.

"I request that the court issue a fair verdict going beyond the Eichmann case and like the judgment of Solomon that it show the world the wisdom of the Jewish people. Proscription is accepted by Jewish tradition and will wipe away the shame of the kidnapping. I therefore request that the court close the case and give the defendant his freedom."

The debate has ended. It is 2:20 p.m. Eichmann wrote yet another note on a piece of paper that he carefully placed in a folder and smiled at his guards. Servatius shook hands with prosecutor Hausner and was talking to the other members of the prosecutor's team. A festive feeling came over the courtroom as it began to empty after the judges had gone. Presiding Judge Landau announced that the sessions would resume in November when the verdict would be made public.

* * *

In summing up four months of hearings we must say that Landau was the perfect presiding judge: he never lost his calm demeanor; with a smile but a firm hand he managed to move the hearings through many difficult moments. Some have criticized him for having limited testimony to the strict minimum too often. They say he didn't understand that this was perhaps the last opportunity for a historical reconstruction of the massacre of the European Jews. But, in spite of the slightly unreal atmosphere of the blue neon lights in the small theater,

Landau didn't forget that he was first and foremost the presiding judge of a court sitting in judgment of one man, one man alone. According to Israeli law the defendant was only a man whose guilt the prosecution was under the obligation to prove. Therefore he didn't spare the prosecution his irony and in one case he may even have gone too far when he curtly called a witness to order because his testimony was turning into a political statement.

Landau was always very correct toward the defense; he listened patiently to the objections that Servatius would come up with from time to time. He always made sure that the defense received the documents introduced by the prosecution in good time and also agreed to consider some of the requests made by him. The most important one being the memoir that Eichmann dictated to the newsman Sassen, which had been obtained by the prosecution amid many difficulties and was accepted only in part by the court. Always attentive to every detail, Landau was often correcting the official interpreter, showing his perfect knowledge not just of Hebrew and German but of other languages as well.

Benjamin Halevy, the judge *a latere*, was supposed to have been the chief justice of the court. He is an iron-willed man who looks young at fifty-one and still has his two children, now university students, shaking in fear. He has been the chief justice of the Jerusalem District Court since 1948, a position that according to the procedure used until a few months ago gave him the right to preside over the court that was to hear the Eichmann case. But to avoid such an outcome Parliament approved a law in January 1961 giving the chief justice position to a judge of the Supreme Court in the event the death penalty was imposed.

The doubts voiced about Halevy came from the fact that he had been the judge in Kastner's trial seven years ago and had described him as being "sold to the devil," meaning to Eichmann, because of the contacts he had during the rescue attempt. That verdict brought about the fall of the Israeli government in 1955 when its general Zionist backers abstained during a confidence vote in parliament. This had cast a shadow not just on Kastner but on his party, the Mapai, as well, even though the verdict was later reversed by the high court.

Halevy's notoriety comes from other famous trials in Israel. He was appointed to the rank of colonel to preside over the court martial that heard the case of the officers and soldiers guilty of the massacre of Kfar Kassem. During the curfew ordered in 1956 on the eve of the Sinai campaign, a few officers and border guard soldiers had killed over a dozen Arab citizens who remained in the camps beyond the time limit. Halevy had already passed judgment at the time regarding the so-called inviolability of superior orders and he found the soldiers guilty even though they had followed the orders of their officers because "the order was clearly illegal."

During the four months of the trial, Halevy seemed to be following the same line as in the controversial Kastner trial. Some witnesses, such as Joel Brand, had also appeared at that time. As the symbol of an absolute, cold, and, I would even venture to say, pitiless justice, Halevy often questioned the witnesses about the delicate issue of Jewish collaboration with the Nazis even when it was forced. At other times he tried to shed light on the part played by the leaders of the Jewish Agency in the rescue of the Jews during the war.

The third judge, Dr. Yitzhak Raveh, listened mostly in silence, holding his chin with such a serious and intent expression on his face that some Italian dailies published his picture mistakenly identifying him as Eichmann. His short questions were actually meant to clarify numbers and statistics in an effort to keep the administrative side of the massacre under control.

Attorney general and prosecutor Gideon Hausner was boring at times, especially at the start of the trial when he mentioned innumerable legal precedents to answer the objections raised by Servatius. But he was always very well informed and logical, and his opening statement remains undoubtedly his masterpiece.

Once Hausner got into the details of the documents that Eichmann knew so well, he was unable to break the defendant. However, he did manage to broaden the scope of the trial by bringing in almost the entire history of that tragic period. The testimony, such as that given by Zuckerman on the Warsaw ghetto, or by Kovner on the Jewish partisans, is essential even though not directly connected to the defendant. On the other hand, few of those testifying could say that they had direct contact with Eichmann or had with their own eyes seen him kill. The disappearance of the Gestapo's central archive was very helpful to the defendant and forced the prosecution to assemble a myriad of documents to reconstruct lost files and correspondence. This was a very difficult task that the prosecution was able to complete, thanks to excellent team work.

Robert Servatius was not an aggressive defense attorney; he limited his input to a few objections and then silently enjoyed the small tactical successes he managed to obtain. He let most of the documents be introduced with his usual *Keine Frage* (no questions), to underscore the fact that he didn't view them as pertinent to the trial. Nevertheless he did object to some specific documents. Eichmann's signature or the initials "IV B4" does appear on some documents, which would clearly guarantee the gallows for the defendant.

Sunday, December 10

Four months have passed since the *Beit Haam* closed its doors, one month more than Landau had estimated to be necessary to reach a verdict. Journalists and detectives greet each other after the long interruption, just like relatives reuniting following a vacation.

On Friday night Eichmann was returned to his cell on the top floor of the *Beit Haam*. Upon his arrival in a police van the preparations for the resumption of the trial were also completed. Tomorrow morning at 9, Judge Landau will read the verdict which he completed this morning. He came personally to the *Beit Haam* to check on the translation into German and English, which along with the French translation will be distributed to the journalists tomorrow as he reads the text in court.

The People's Hall has seen no changes. The high metal fence surrounding the building has been moved back, letting normal city traffic to flow in the surrounding streets while it had been blocked during the initial phase of the trial. The closed circuit television screens allowing the public and newsmen to view the proceedings from the press room and a second classroom are also gone. The American company having the exclusive rights to the filming was no longer involved, so a local outfit will now film the sessions with regular cameras.

Eichmann has spent the last few days with his defense attorney who returned to Israel ten days ago. They agreed to the text of Eichmann's final statement before the verdict is to be read. This morning the police doctor examined him in his cell and found him to be in good health. He spent the four intervening months writing his memoirs, which he finished a few days ago. Servatius after failing to have the Bonn government pay for his services, will now attempt to get the Israeli government to allow him retain the proceeds from the publication of the Eichmann memoirs.

The Israeli population hasn't shown much interest so far in the resumption of the trial. The few people who walk past the *Beit Haam* go by quickly without lingering. No small groups, no demonstrations of any kind. For the Israelis the trial was over several months ago, ever since the prosecution revealed the gigantic scope of the Nazi crimes to the world. But as the court reconvenes the discussion about the sentence Eichmann should receive has begun anew.

Martin Buber, the most widely known Jewish philosopher, is over eighty and lives in Jerusalem. He stated that if the death penalty is handed down he will ask the president of Israel for a commutation because: "The commandment 'thou shall not kill' is absolute and applies to the state as well as to individuals." He is the author of many books about Hassidism, a mystical Jewish movement of the 18th century. He was in the news as one of the first Israelis to appear at a public event in Germany right after the war. He now is part of various pacifist movements, prompting a joke that Israel's problem is that philosophers are in politics while statesmen like Ben Gurion are involved in philosophy…

Professor Hugo Bergman, another eminent philosopher and former dean of the University of Jerusalem, issued a statement a few days ago with the same ideas as Buber's in light of Judaism's ethical principles.

However, Buber and Bergman are not Israel. They belong to a tiny intellectual élite that is widely respected but doesn't represent the country. What does the man in the street really think about the Eichmann verdict?

We first asked a bus driver. "Before the trial I must confess that I knew almost nothing about Nazism. The Nazis never made it to Iraq. But now, after reading for months on end what was going on in the trial, I have some idea about the crimes committed. How could I even imagine that he could be allowed to live? Are we to provide for him after all he had done?"

Eitan is a young university student fresh out of the army. "For me the trial explained how six million Jews were butchered without reacting. Without a major revolt. Now I think I understand. Perhaps it would have been simpler to have eliminated him in Argentina, but then my friends and I would have never learned the truth. But I don't see why he should be pardoned now. He committed crimes and he must pay."

Hannah is a housewife who spends her days tending to her children. "I don't know much about the law and criminal court procedure. One thing I do know: my parents and all my relatives died at Auschwitz. And it was Eichmann who deported them out of Hungary. It is an insult to their memory to ask for pity for such a beast. The death penalty in my view is the bare minimum he should receive. First he should be reduced to a living skeleton like those at Auschwitz—" She stops, overcome by emotion.

Aharon is a government employee. "I don't understand why the so-called civilized world is getting so excited about saving a criminal from the gallows. That same world watched in silence while my three brothers were murdered. Today they are talking about Eichmann's family, about his wife, his children. But no one seems to want to hear about the children who were killed. They wanted a regular trial with all the trimmings of due process. So therefore the death penalty is the logical consequence."

The nuances and the motivations change according to the person who is questioned, but their answers all have a common denominator. For Eichmann the only penalty can be death.

Monday, December 11

Using an exceptional proceeding Judge Landau announced at the beginning of the session that Eichmann had been found guilty.

According to customary procedure the judges declare the defendant guilty or not of the crimes he is accused of only after reading the motives for the verdict. Today's announcement didn't surprise anyone, not even Eichmann.

Wearing his neatly pressed shirt with his striped tie and the same suit as four months ago, his thinning hair carefully combed, Eichmann looks a lot better that when we last saw him in August. At that time he had been subjected to a long and exhausting cross-examination by the prosecutor. Now he appears to be returning from summer vacation. Only his complexion, that the neon lighting makes even more pale, and his uninterrupted blinking betray his nervous tension. This is understandable, since Israeli law allows the death penalty for crimes against the Jewish people, against humanity, and for war crimes, all of which he was found guilty of. Today's announcement is therefore tantamount to the death penalty.

Even today the public showed little interest. Perhaps it was this morning's rain and wind that kept the expected crowd away from the entrance of the police office where the two hundred passes for the public are handed out. The fate of Eichmann the man is of no interest to the Israelis. It is important that for the first time in the history of the Jewish people it brought at least one of its murderers to justice for attempting to exterminate it. "We are no longer a people fated to be slaughtered," writes one newspaper today. "We are a sovereign people capable of judging those who persecuted us."

"The court finds you guilty of crimes against the Jewish people, crimes against humanity, war crimes, and of membership in criminal organizations." With these few words that Eichmann listened to while standing, Judge Landau opened this morning's hearing. The defendant was then allowed to sit down while the judge began reading the prologue of the long sentence.

"What distinguishes this trial is that for the first time the murder of the Jewish people is the main focus of court proceedings. Many questions remain unanswered: How could such a mass murder take place so openly? Would the Nazis have been able to carry out their crimes without the collaboration of the people among whom the Jews were living? Could at least part of the massacre have been avoided had the

Allies been more forceful in saving those who were being persecuted? What are the deeper roots of anti-Semitism and which lesson should the people draw from what has taken place?

"The court, however, was determined to not slide into matters that didn't concern it. We have not been asked to pronounce our judgment on the fundamental issues that do not belong to the realm of the law where our opinion would carry far less weight than that of any other scholar."

Before getting into the sentencing proper, the court had to answer the issue of its own legal competence to stand in judgment of Adolf Eichmann, which Servatius had questioned at the beginning of the trial. Judge Halevy read this strictly technical part filled with quotations in four languages. "The objection that our law is retroactive and therefore illegal is without merit since the Nazis knew that they were perpetrating criminal acts, as their efforts to erase all traces can attest. The defendant is accused of having followed a plan for the 'final solution' of the Jewish problem. Could anyone in his right mind possibly doubt the criminal nature of such actions? Even the 'reason of state' cannot exonerate the individual from his responsibilities, as was already established by the Regulations of the Nuremberg Tribunal and later approved by the Assembly of the United Nations. From the point of view of international law the competence of the court derives from the universal character of the crimes committed, which gives every state the right to judge and punish the crimes in question. The relationship between the State of Israel and those crimes is no less important where the victim is the Jewish people. The people as victim is fully within its rights to stand in judgment of those who were attempting to exterminate it. There is a tangible connection between the State of Israel that was created and recognized as a 'Jewish state' and the Jewish people.

"If, as the defense asserts, the only valid principle would be the territorial principle, then some eighteen countries would also have every right to punish the defendant for the murder of the Jews residing in their territory. However, if the victims were part of the nation, they wouldn't have such a right since they were not exterminated on a land of their own. A people that can be exterminated at will views its very existence as being in constant in danger. Any criminal could assault the

Jewish people without fear of punishment. This was the curse of being in exile. But now the sovereign Jewish state has the power to punish the assassins who carried out Hitler's infamous projects."

At the end of the indictment Judge Raveh began reading the actual sentence that follows in chronological order the various phases of the anti-Semitic persecutions and indicates the role played by the defendant. By reordering the huge mass of documents and testimony presented before by the prosecution, the sentence gives a summary of Nazi activity in the different countries. It restates how Eichmann, beginning as a low-level official in the intelligence service, was incrementally given executive responsibilities at the time he set up the central office for emigration in Vienna. Through sheer terror he managed to get 150,000 Austrian Jews to emigrate, while relieving them of all their possessions. He returned to Berlin covered in glory. It is not surprising that he was promoted to a central role in the war against the Jews.

The sentence then describes the second phase of the persecutions, from the moment Germany went to war in September 1939 to the invasion of Russia in 1941, that was marked by mass deportations. Eichmann's task was to organize the transports into Poland. Without a shadow of compassion he not only was involved in transportation but also in the round-ups. The Madagascar Plan, which the defendant had the impudence of stating that it came from his reading of Herzl, was actually meant to isolate the Jews into a slave state.

The third and final phase of the persecutions began with the war against the Soviet Union and the total extermination policy. It is based upon documents and testimony from the Wannsee Conference of January 1942, showing the part that Eichmann played. It examines the defendant's activities in each European country under Nazi occupation and cites the opposition of Italian troops as one of the main obstacles to his anti-Semitic fury in France, Corsica, and Greece. In those three areas of Italian occupation deportations only became possible after September 8, 1943. The order to deport the Jews of Rome in October 1943 was issued by Himmler. In his deposition, Kappler stated that Dannecker was the only one responsible. It is obvious that both Kappler and Dannecker took part in the raid in Rome on October 16,

1943, and that they were acting on the basis of orders from RSHA, of which Dannecker was a part. After the liberation of Mussolini the Italian republican government decided to assemble the Jews in concentration camps. The internees were for the most part deported to Auschwitz or other camps and to their death.

Hungary, the sentence goes on to state, was of special importance to the defendant since he left his Berlin office to go to Budapest with his staff. After recalling the deportations and the tragic "march on foot," the judges examined the role played by Eichmann in the negotiations of "supplies for blood." It is entirely hypocritical to say today that the failure of the negotiations brought about in Eichmann the same kind of anger and fury as in Joel Brand. Eichmann was, on the contrary, quite pleased about it. The defendant was the linchpin of the "final solution" in Hungary and since he was on location he displayed even more initiative, energy, and the ability to take bold action."

To speed up the reading of the sentence, the presiding judge has decided to add a third evening session. Before moving on to the chapter concerning the death camps, the judges question the degree to which Eichmann took part in the actual extermination operations. "We feel that this issue is only of secondary importance, since the legal and moral responsibility of the person sending the victim to his death is no less great from our point of view than the responsibility of the person who kills with his own hands and may in fact even be greater."

Tuesday, December 12

The reading of the verdict proceeds slowly, going from the boring minutiae to the extreme; the accountant of death is being served an accurate ledger of his crimes. Or at least of those crimes that the judges hold to be proven beyond a reasonable doubt. Some people have actually acquitted Eichmann for insufficient evidence, as for example in the killing of the Jewish boy who had stolen some cherries in the garden of his villa in Budapest.

Such detail certainly conforms to the Anglo-Saxon legal tradition upon which most of the Israeli criminal code is modeled, but it can leave us a bit disappointed. It almost appears that the mountain has given birth to a mouse. Everything in the Jerusalem courtroom is clean, scrubbed, and sterilized; the smell of corpses, the smoke of the crematoria, the final cries of those choking to death in the gas chambers are absent. The sentence and the crimes are out of proportion and not only is drama absent but even a heartfelt and manly condemnation of the defendant and his superiors. The judges appear to be endowed with a detached kind of objectivity, allowing them to coldly establish that Eichmann was in fact responsible for the sterilization of Jewish women at Theresienstadt but not at Kovno, and that he is considered guilty of the crime detailed in paragraph 3b of the indictment but not of the one in paragraph 3d. We can only listen to the droning voices of the judges who alternate in reading the sentence that is filled with quotations like a treatise in legal history.

But this may also strengthen the sentence itself. Devoid of any rhetorical effects it shall remain a legal document to be transmitted to future generations. The only strength the victims may have is contained in the law and it is the only weapon they may use, even against those like Eichmann who is guilty of unbelievable crimes.

Today's portion of the sentence examines Eichmann's role in the extermination. He knew as of August 1941 that the deportations were meant to kill the Jews and he therefore was with that knowledge sending them to die. He also took part in the meetings when it was decided to substitute the shootings with the exhaust fumes. He had to have been aware of the role of his deputy, Günther, in the supply of Zyklon-B gas.

"Eichmann has given us an odd self-portrait. As head of a section of the RSHA with a rank equivalent to that of colonel, with many councilors for Jewish Affairs in many countries who depended upon him, the defendant would have us believe that in such a position he would have limited himself to the strict, piecemeal execution of orders as he received them while his subordinates enjoyed the widest possible initiative and that Günther would even take action behind Eichmann's back. But the testimony we have heard proves, on the contrary, that the defendant had within RSHA a position that in no way corresponds to his version according to which he hadn't the smallest influence after 1941. We are not facing a low-level, small-time, meticulous civil servant, but a man who acts according to his will and is aware of his power to the point that he didn't even consider an order from the Führer as being final.

"This doesn't contradict in any way Eichmann's desire to always be 'covered.' But as soon as he was 'covered' by a preceding order he would take action without clearing it with anyone. He constantly repeated that he had only been busy preparing train schedules for the deportees. But in truth his main job was not to provide the trains but rather the Jews. Eichmann was not a puppet being led around by others: he was among those who were pulling the strings.

"The 'final solution' was a vast and complex operation that cannot be parceled neatly into sections. Therefore, those who knowingly took part in it must be considered accomplices in the murder of millions of people. The responsibility becomes much greater as we move away from the actual perpetrators, since the real instigators were in higher positions.

"The defendant's main defense rests on the claim that he was merely executing orders from his superiors and that his entire up-bringing led him to believe that blind obedience was a supreme duty. But the law doesn't accept such a justification and the defendant cannot escape from his responsibility for the crimes that were committed even if he carried them out as orders coming from the authorities. The defendant was aware that the order for the physical extermination of the Jews was very clearly illegal and that in carrying it out he was committing a crime. The disciplinary rules of the SS provided that those who executed criminal orders would be punished.

"Eichmann never showed any pity for the victims. On the contrary, he was an enthusiastic executioner, a fanatical Nazi deeply convinced that he was accomplishing an important national mission. But blind obedience wouldn't have been enough; the key positions he held required a lot of initiative, thinking, and organizational skill. The defendant was therefore entirely dedicated to his action and was happy to have done good work by sending the Jews to their death. At the end of the war he expressed his satisfaction for having killed five million Jews.

"Naturally the defendant was no exception. He was a faithful official of a regime of criminals. It is impossible to draw a complete picture without mentioning the other leaders who were also responsible. Hitler and the Nazi leadership; the Ministries of the Interior and Justice that provided the formal basis for the persecutions, facilitating Eichmann's mission; the Ministry of Foreign Affairs that spread the anti-Semitic poison worldwide; and that of Finance, which took part in the looting; the German army's High Command, which collaborated with the SS. And not only them, but all the officials of the Reich who were competing among themselves to exterminate the Jews quickly and completely. But all this doesn't erase the fact that Eichmann and his section played a key role in the murder of the Jews and the crimes associated with those murders and in no way diminishes the defendant's responsibility.

"The defendant's testimony is an accumulation of lies in spite of his repeated declarations to only wish to tell the truth, and tends to reduce his responsibility as much as possible.

"The court therefore finds Eichmann guilty of all fifteen counts of the indictment."

Eichmann listened to the sentence looking like someone without either any compassion or conscience; calm and detached, he looked at the judges as his eyes moved to the left, away from the audience. The metal pillar of his glass booth projects a shadow over his face. Some have compared it to the branding iron used by the Jews to mark murderers.

Wednesday, December 13

Today's session, one of the shortest of this trial, shall remain one of the most important. According to Israeli procedure once the guilt of the defendant is established the prosecution and the defense again address the degree of punishment to be applied. The defendant has the right to speak at the end and the judges finally meet in chambers to discuss the verdict and set the sentence.

The prosecutor had some intensely dramatic moments today in his summation, in contrast with the rigidly legalistic reading of the sentence. Today's speech was one of Hausner's most brilliant addresses, equal almost to his opening statement of eight months ago.

"By now everything has been said in this trial. I would not want to add anything to the testimony of the survivors who recalled the ocean of blood and tears that shall always live in our hearts. For the one who day after day, was for years at the center of the diabolical work of extermination with cruelty and dedication, there may only be one kind of punishment."

The prosecutor went on to state that capital punishment is the only one for such cases, according to Israeli law, and not the maximum one.

"For the horrors that were committed Eichmann has banished himself from the rest of humanity. Thirsty for blood like a hyena, he crossed the line that divides men from beasts. The worst killer remains a human being. But someone who attempts to murder an entire people under the influence of a cold and calculating hatred places himself outside humanity.

"Eichmann has no right to your pity, your honors, because his heart showed none at all. His only regret is to have left some Jews alive in Hungary.

"His defense lawyer may object that the statute of limitations comes into play. But there is no possible redemption for the blood of millions that cries out, overflowing, and demands that justice be done. Sixteen years have passed but even all the way to the last generations we cannot forget. The void created by the death of over one million children cannot be filled for centuries. This is the reason why Eichmann's crime lives on today in the fullest of its horror. The crimes of the Nazis are not dry material for studies by historians; they are with us today as never before. Nazism has not disappeared in the world and its seeds are still filled with life. It must be made clear to all that whoever is guilty of crimes like Eichmann's has no right to mitigating circumstances. I therefore ask that the court inflict the only punishment that civil society imposes on the worst criminals, even though it is a modest punishment for what he has done.

"Some have said that since it is impossible to impose a punishment that is proportionate to the magnitude of the crimes, the death penalty should be avoided. Yes, no punishment in the world can balance the actions taken by the defendant in a single day. But is this enough to make it impossible for us to act in the face of such crimes?

"It's true that by executing a single Nazi, even someone like Eichmann, we will not balance the loss of blood. The wound is too deep for it to heal. The loss will never be recovered and as long as there is one Jew left on the earth he will not forget what was done to our people. Eichmann didn't act alone: he could count on battalions of criminals who collaborated with him and many of them have not been punished. However, among the Nazis who are alive, Eichmann is a central figure in the mechanism of extermination. If he doesn't pay with the penalty of death, who else will it be used against? For the enemy of humankind, for the murderer of the Jewish people who sits in front of you here, I request the death penalty."

Hausner has finished. In one hour, without rhetorical flourishes but with great vigor he managed to place the trial in its proper perspective by recalling the enormity of the crimes that Eichmann had committed. The penalty he requested didn't appear to be an act of vengeance but the only one that was legally and morally possible. Even though it is inadequate it remains the minimum and the maximum that civil society can impose.

Servatius then claimed that the defendant did not act out of his own initiative but according to orders from his superiors. "Today the people who are responsible in the face of history have abandoned the defendant in this courtroom to be the scapegoat. Only the leadership is responsible and what happened to the German people could happen to any other people.

"But the defendant's actions shall not be continued. The death penalty would therefore not have any educational value and the purpose of this trial has already been reached by finding him guilty. The Bible says that punishment and vengeance belong to our Lord. It is therefore within grace and charity that our problems shall find a solution; I ask that the judges consider this when they impose the penalty."

Servatius appeared colorless, dry and unconvincing. Not only because he was pleading a lost cause from the start, but because he decided to let his client answer the indictment. Once his turn came, Eichmann stood up, switched his glasses to a new pair that he took out of his coat pocket and opened the file he was carrying from his cell.

"I understand the heavy sentence that the court has issued. My hopes of finding justice have been frustrated. The depositions by the witnesses who came here have made my blood curdle in the same way as when I was compelled to watch those horrors myself. I had the misfortune of getting mixed up in those horrors, but they were not the result of what I wanted. I never intended to kill human beings. Only the political leadership can be held responsible for this mass murder. My fault was in my obedience and loyalty to the oath and to the flag. I didn't persecute the Jews out of passion or for pleasure as the government was doing.

"I accuse the government leaders of abusing my obedience, the very obedience which at the time was considered a virtue. The leadership group to which I did not belong deserved to be punished. But the subordinates are victims and I am one of them.

"It was impossible for me at that time to go against the orders I was given. But it is a mistake to say that I was a fanatic in the persecutions of the Jews, even though my superiors placed the blame on me.

"No one, not even the Reverend Gruber, who came to me asking for clemency, accused me regarding my activities. At the Ministry of the Interior Loessner was aware of the atrocities and had discussed them with his superiors. No one, however, had any objections. That was the degree of civic courage that could be found in a high official.

"The Governor General of Poland, Hans Frank, and Rudolf Höss, the commandant at Auschwitz, had every reason to plead guilty. But I am in a different situation. I never had the responsibilities of someone like Frank nor did I commit mass murder like Höss. Had they ordered me to do so, I would have shot myself.

"The court has judged my attitude as being false. But it was impossible for me to remember every detail. I did not remain silent as the 3,500 pages of the reports indicate. I made some mistakes and I should have been given the opportunity to correct myself.

"I can only examine my conscience. But from the legal point of view, I am innocent.

"If I could, I would now ask the Jewish people for forgiveness. But this would be viewed as pure hypocrisy on my part. I am not a monster; I am the victim of a mistaken conclusion.

"In Buenos Aires I was assaulted and held tied to a bed for a week. Obviously I am held responsible for everything since some Nazis have wanted to exonerate themselves at my expense. I am deeply convinced that I am being made to pay here for the actions of others. All I can do is accept what fate is imposing upon me."

A heavy silence fell over the courtroom. Eichmann has passed up the final opportunity to express some form of contrition. At the end of each typed page he would pause, stop reading for a few seconds, and signal the interpreter to translate his words into Hebrew. His eyes would move from the prosecutor to the judges and then to the interpreter. Never to the audience. To the end Eichmann wanted to be the director of the film of his role in this horrible carnage. Instead, Hausner's words come back to memory as he said them shortly before: "Eichmann crossed the barrier that separates human beings from beasts." Whether he is a beast or not, it is clear that he is on a different wavelength than our own. To the end he is insisting on hiding behind the absurd screen of superior orders. He is disappointed by the verdict; the witnesses were lying; his superiors betrayed him. He is left to pay for something he didn't do.

He has finished. He carefully closes his folder and sits down, back straight. The play is over and the curtain may fall on this stage.

At 9 a.m. on the day after tomorrow, the judges will almost certainly condemn him to death. Then the entire complex death penalty procedure will begin for Eichmann.

For the past seven years the death penalty is no longer part of regular Israeli legislation and was kept only for Nazi crimes. But even during the first years of the State of Israel no death sentence had ever been carried out. There was no clear procedure in this area and it became necessary to return to British mandate regulations while making the needed changes. According to those rules the condemned is dressed in red immediately following the verdict and transferred in handcuffs, with chains on his feet, to the "central prison of Acco or Jerusalem."

However, the prisons no longer exist, so Eichmann will be taken to the jail at Rambe. Even though a recent law stipulates that the death penalty will be carried out by hanging, there is now the issue of the gallows. It doesn't exist in Israel. Acco prison, now turned into an insane asylum, has one that is kept as a museum piece because the British used it to execute the Jewish terrorists of the *Irgun Zwai Leumi*. Many Israelis will object that it should be used to hang Eichmann so a new gallows must be built. The law states that the day before the execution it should be examined by a police official and a public works engineer to make sure it works. To check the rope, a bag as heavy as the defendant is tied to it. The execution must take place in secret before 8 in the morning and, under the mandate, a black flag had to be raised on the roof of the jail.

If Eichmann is hanged the major issue will be what to do with his body. Will the family want it? And will the executioner have to be recruited through a competitive selection as the law requires in hiring state employees?

Mr. Eichmann creates many problems. It is even difficult to get rid of him.

Friday, December 15, 1961

Upon entering the courtroom this morning we thought we were going to witness a formality, a film we already knew, having previously read the script. But while the death penalty was long expected even the 121st and final hearing of the trial had some highly dramatic moments.

A few minutes before 9 a.m. the courtroom is filled with newsmen and the small number of the audience that managed, after a long wait in line under the rain, to secure passes to get in. Many others remained outside and are staying close to the gates with their transistor radios in hand to follow the verdict as it is being broadcast. In the front row are the officials of the "06" section who prepared the preliminary investigation. The entire prosecution team is present in the courtroom. Next to the public prosecutor, Gideon Hausner, sits Dr. Jacob Robinson, the international law expert who served as the councilor to the prosecutor; and the deputy prosecutors Yakov Bar-Or and Gabriel Bach. The defense attorney, Robert Servatius, has the young lawyer Dieter Wechtenbruch at his side. Eichmann is brought into his glass booth and before sitting down he nods at his defense attorney. His mouth twists from time to time in one of his well-known grimaces. Everything is ready; but the chairs to be used by the judges placed under the state seal (a menorah) remain empty.

Minutes go by slowly. Tension is mounting in the courtroom. The same audience that Judge Landau had to call to silence so many times now sits perfectly quiet and in heavy expectation. It is the first time that the judges are late. Perhaps the unusual delay is due to a final check of the translation of the verdict that they are about to pronounce. Eichmann sits motionless, and as usual doesn't condescend to glance in our direction.

Finally, at 9:17 a.m., the usher announces *Beit Hamishpat* and the judges enter the courtroom. They look pale and tired, with circles under their eyes, attesting to scores of sleepless nights. Judge Landau asks the defendant to stand and begins reading the verdict. His voice is a bit shaky. When he states, "We have considered the punishment, deeply aware of the responsibility that rests with us," he is certainly convincing. He appears to be more emotional than Eichmann himself.

In a short prologue, the verdict states first of all that it is up to the court to decide the punishment since the death penalty is not, as the prosecution stated, the only one possible by law. Landau then said: "We have examined the case and have reached the conclusion that we shall apply the maximum penalty. The destruction of an entire people and the crimes against humanity are huge crimes that surpass in their severity the sum of the single criminal acts they are made of. We must also consider the suffering inflicted upon the victims and their relatives, who feel the consequences to this day. Every train of one thousand human beings that the defendant dispatched to Auschwitz represents his direct participation in one thousand murders and his legal and moral responsibility is no less great than that of those who ushered them into the gas chambers with their own hands.

"Had we found that the defendant, as he claims, acted out of blind obedience, we would also say that he must be inflicted the harshest punishment, since there are no mitigating circumstances for someone who for years took part in crimes of such proportions. But we have found, on the contrary, that the defendant wholeheartedly approved the orders he was given and was able to fully endorse their criminal purpose.

"This court condemns Adolf Eichmann to the penalty of death for crimes against the Jewish people, against humanity, and the war crimes he was found guilty of. This is the verdict."

It is 9:25 a.m. The reading has lasted less than ten minutes. The presiding judge explains to the defendant that it is his right to make an appeal to the High Court of Justice within ten days. He reminded the defense attorney that he may ask for an extension to that deadline. The final words that were uttered in court during the legal proceedings were ironically to be those of defense attorney Servatius, who thanked the presiding judge.

 After eight months of sessions and eighteen months following the capture of the former SS colonel, the Eichmann trial has ended. His death will not close the books on the tragedy of the Jewish people at the hands of Nazi Germany. The punishment inflicted upon him is out of proportion with the enormity of the crimes he has committed. But it is the only possible outcome and it must serve as a warning for the entire world.

It may be difficult to express a comprehensive opinion today and determine whether this was an historical trial or simply another court proceeding against an individual SS officer. The prosecution always tried to broaden the horizon while the judges had to narrow it instead. But, undoubtedly, the trial shall remain a permanent monument to the memory of the victims of Nazism. The words used by Hausner at the start of his opening statement come back to mind: "When I stand up to speak inside this courtroom, six million dead persons are with me and I must be their spokesman…"

Publisher's Note

Adolf Eichmann was hanged on May 31, 1962, in Jerusalem.

Postscript

The fiftieth anniversary of the Eichmann trial has received renewed attention in Israel. Panel discussions and new books underscore its importance and the repercussions it still has on Israeli society. Today the past is seen in a new light.

Some commentators are convinced that then Prime Minister David Ben Gurion wanted the trial to take place for a number of reasons.

First, there was the desire to erase the bitter taste of the legal action taken and lost by Israel Kastner in 1954–55. The trial showed that the leaders of Mapai only took limited initiatives in attempting to save the Jews of Europe.

Then there was the political need to counterbalance the bad impression created by the sale of Israeli small arms to West Germany that caused the fall of the government in 1959. And also perhaps to have the public forget the riots of Wadi Salib in Haifa in 1959 that revealed for the first time the divisions between oriental and western Jews.

The main motivation, however, was the educational value the trial would have for Israeli youth, so that it may understand what had happened during the *Shoah* and make sure that nothing of the sort could take place again in the future.

On May 23, 1960, David Ben Gurion announced in the Knesset that Adolf Eichmann had been arrested, was being held in an Israeli prison, and that he would stand trial.

I happened to be traveling through Rome at the time and was able to ask Argentine president Arturo Frondizi a few questions that were broadcast on Israeli radio. Naturally he condemned the kidnapping. The announcement of the upcoming trial also prompted me to publish a report on the event; the publisher Longanesi expressed an interest.

Eichmann played an important part in the implementation of the extermination policy even though he tried very hard to convince everyone that the opposite was true. His entire defense position was based on his claim that he was nothing but a lowly civilian official steeped in bureaucratic routine and intent on carrying out orders.

As I wrote at the time: "By constantly repeating that his duty of obedience was devoid of any kind of moral considerations whatsoever, Eichmann provides us with the portrait of the perfect Nazi civil servant, as someone who remains true to his mission, and is capable of transporting the Jews to the death camps just as easily as he would convey shipments of potatoes to the army's warehouses."

Some years ago Hanna Yablonka published a book that examines in detail the effect of the trial on Israeli society. For many death camp survivors it was almost therapeutic and perhaps for the first time in Israel, society at large could identify with the victims of the *Shoah*. Before the trial the only real victims were thought to be those murdered by the Nazis and there was some criticism in the formula that was fashionable at the time that "they went like a herd of sheep to the slaughter."

After the verdict it became clear that the survivors were also victims, and that some had resisted and fought, for example as Jewish partisans, and that the *Yshuv,* or the Jewish population in Palestine at that time, could have done more to attempt to save its European brothers and sisters. The survivors therefore acquired greater prestige and could stop justifying themselves while the older Israelis discovered a renewed interest in the heart wrenching accounts of the *Shoah*. The result was that the *Shoah* became part of the national memory and the collective consciousness.

Furthermore, the feeling that this must never happen again under any circumstances fortified the political will to defend the State of Israel behind secure and recognized borders. Yablonka rightly underlines the fact that public opinion was influenced more by the witnesses testifying at the trial than by any other aspect of the proceedings.

A few scholars have attempted to examine the impact in 1961 of the Eichmann trial on Italian public opinion. Manuela Consonni writes that the trial played an important part in lifting the veil of silence and forgetfulness regarding the Nazi concentration camps.[18] However Consonni doesn't take into account the key factor of radio and television. RAI (Radio Televisione Italiana) was broadcasting my two-minute report on the daily trial sessions every evening along with fifty seconds on television news. I remember arriving in Italy for a brief visit after the trial and going into a retail store to hear the lady at the cash register recognize my voice because she was hearing it every evening on radio.

Besides the broadcast media that was reaching a large audience, I was also writing a series of illustrated articles for the large circulation newsweekly *L'Espresso,* then edited by Arrigo Benedetti. The points I was making were focusing on the idea, which was prevalent at the time, of a Jewish resistance. I remember one report entitled "For Forty Days We Were An Army," about my interview with Yitzhak Zuckerman, who had led the Warsaw ghetto uprising.

A self-hating comment did come from Idit Zertal, for whom "the infinite repetition" that a new *Shoah* was bound to happen in Israel is the expression of "an isolated nation surrounded by an anti-Semitic world as an eternal victim." [19]

As Georges Bensoussan writes,[20] Israel can speak for the Jews of the world since the Nazis had murdered the Jews as a people. Bensoussan also points to the "Christian uneasiness" making it difficult to accept a trial resulting from a kidnapping that was held in front of an Israeli rather than an international court and in Jerusalem of all places, the city of Jewish redemption and of Christian triumph.

This last point is particularly important. Pope Pius XII had also assigned to the Catholic Church the role of victim of the Nazis. On June 2, 1945, a few days after the end of the Second World War in Europe, he gave a speech to the cardinals on the occasion of the feast day of his namesake, Saint Eugene. He was defending the Concordat he had signed with the Nazi Reich in 1933, claiming that it was

---

18. Manuela Consonni, "The Impact of the Eichmann Event in Italy," 1961, *Journal of Israeli History,* n. 23 (2004), pp. 90–99, Special Edition: "After Eichmann: Collective Memory and the Holocaust Since 1961," eds. D. Cesarani and A. Shapira, London, Frank Cass
19. Idit Zertal, *Israele e la Shoà, la nazione e il culto della tragedia,* Giulio Einaudi editore, Torino, 2007, pp. 117-118.
20. Georges Bensoussan, *Israele un nome eterno, Lo Stato d' Israele, il sionismo e lo sterminio degli Ebrei d'Europa,* UTET, 2009, Torino, p. 123-135

intended to secure guarantees for the German Catholics. He reaffirmed "the incompatibility between National Socialist ideas and Christian doctrine" while National Socialism was denouncing "the Church as the enemy of the German people." This was "the clearest and most honorable evidence of the firm, and constantly upheld opposition on the part of the Church." He stated that "the National Socialist hostility toward the Church" intended "to do away with the Church once and for all."[21] According to Andrea Riccardi, Pius XII claimed that the Church never lent its support to Nazism, and actually "can be placed among those persecuted by them." A statement that in my view doesn't reflect what really happened and is an attempt to rewrite history.[22]

This was the first step toward the Christianization of the *Shoah*, which was later pursued mostly by John Paul II[23] when he spoke at Auschwitz of "six million Poles" as victims, and encouraged the creation of a convent next to the death camp grounds, which after long negotiations was relocated just 500 meters away.

In this English translation of my diary of the trial, I have privileged the testimony of the witnesses, often reproducing exactly what they stated in court. I hope that the impressions that were recorded in the heat of the daily trial proceedings remain just as vivid today.

---

21. Discorso di Sua Santità Pio XII "Nell'accogliere", del 2 giugno 1945. www.vaticano.va.
22. See Andrea Riccardi, "Governo e 'profezia' nel pontificato di Pio XII," in Pio XII, a cura di A. Riccardi, Laterza, 1984, p. 52.
23. Sergio Minerbi, "Pope John II and the Jews: An Evaluation," *Jewish Political Studies Review*, 18:1-2 (Spring 2006).

Index